ACTION STATIONS!

Transforming language learning through creative strategies

Simon Green and Steve Haworth

CiLT | THE NATIONAL CENTRE FOR LANGUAGES

The views expressed in this publication are the authors' and do not necessarily represent those of CILT.

Acknowledgements

The authors would like to acknowledge the debt owed to the following who initially inspired the writing of this book with their concept of *les simulations globales:* Jean-Marc Caré and Francis Debyser. For a fuller treatment of this concept we refer you to *Simulations globales* by Jean-Marc Caré (CIEP, 1997) and *L'immeuble* by Francis Debyser (Hachette,1986).

We should also like to thank the following for their help in the preparation of this book: Marie Doublier, Catherine Cheater, Emma Rees, Teresa Tinsley, David Kennedy.

First published 2003
by the Centre for Information on Language Teaching and Research (CILT)
20 Bedfordbury
London
WC2N 4LB

Illustrations by Richard Duszczak

ISBN 1 904243 07 X

A catalogue record for this book is available from the British Library

Printed in Great Britain by Hobbs

CILT Publications are available from: **Central Books**, 99 Wallis Rd, London E9 5LN. Tel: 0845 458 9910. Fax: 0845 458 9912. Book trade representation (UK and Ireland): **Broadcast Book Services**, Charter House, 27a London Rd, Croydon CR0 2RE. Tel: 020 8681 8949. Fax: 020 8688 0615.

CONTENTS

[P]   All pages marked with this symbol are photocopiable
for use with your students.

INTRODUCTION

The aim of this book is twofold:

- first, to show how a creative approach to language learning may help teachers regain professional independence in the classroom;
- second, to help learners experience success in their language learning endeavours.

We believe that, for teachers to focus on the enjoyment and challenge of learning a language and for pupils to enjoy their language learning in a way that is both intellectually stimulating and of practical use, there needs to be a shift towards a more dynamic pedagogy.

The point is well illustrated by this quotation (Brown 2000):

> *Pedagogy specifically refers to the role of the teacher in bringing a subject alive. (...) Methodology tends to stay on the page, while pedagogy implies a sense of energy; it tells us how the teacher interacts with the methodology to engage pupils in their learning.*

There are external demands upon teachers which prescribe in detail certain curricular requirements:

- Some are statutory (such as the National Curriculum Programme of Study).
- Some are recommended (such as the QCA Scheme of Work for Key Stage 3).
- Some are for guidance (such as the National Literacy Strategy).
- Some are for convenience (such as a particular coursebook).

One of the paradoxes of this situation is that despite the array of advice and prescription that is available to the teacher of Modern Foreign Languages (MFL), OFSTED still report insufficient progress in both key stages of secondary school:

> *The slow improvement in standards of achievement in MFL continues, but pupils' achievement is still lower than in most other subjects. Pupils need to develop further the 'productive' skills of speaking and writing in the foreign language.* (OFSTED report on MFL in secondary schools for 2000/01)

Some pupils have also reported confusion about the precise purpose of some of their modern language lessons:

> *It is disturbing that many of the pupils interviewed had little by way of a clear view of what they were supposed to have learnt from a typical lesson, even in terms, for example, of new words acquired.* (Lee, Buckland and Shaw 1998)

In order to meet these challenges, this book sets out three key objectives:

- To enable teachers to maximise their own time in the classroom to help their pupils learn languages more effectively.
- To offer an approach to language learning which is both intellectually demanding and emotionally satisfying for both teacher and pupil.
- To provide a variety of creative strategies which may be used within existing frameworks or as free-standing modules to help pupils make language learning personal.

This book provides a range of creative strategies to help pupils learn languages more effectively. **It offers:**

- an innovative approach for those in their first years of language learning in secondary school (Key Stage 3 and S1/S2 in Scotland);
- a challenging new strategy for those at an intermediate level (Key Stage 4 and S3/S4 in Scotland);
- activities designed to engage learners;
- a synthesis of good practice;
- motivational techniques for group work;
- a guide to useful resources.

It is **aimed at** all learners in secondary schools and **builds on** the guiding principles of:

- the National Literacy Strategy;
- the Key Stage 3 National Strategy;
- the National Curriculum (MFL) Programme of Study;
- QCA Secondary schemes of work for Modern Foreign Languages.

It is **based on** and **informed by:**

- recent developments in accelerated learning theory;
- brain research;
- Government initiatives on raising standards;
- recent publications on teaching the gifted and talented;
- training courses on creative approaches to teaching MFL given by the authors over the past five years.

The central idea of the book is enhancing individual role plays in the MFL classroom into more extended stories. Instead of discrete, short role plays, the pupils develop an on-going storyline with a number of fictional characters. The key component in these stories is the context in which they are set. This context provides the opportunity for extended speaking and writing. The stories are primarily for performance and pupils derive a good deal of pleasure in acting out their mini dramas for their peers. These performances provide ample opportunity for formative assessment and a good record of pupil achievement.

The extended writing comes through record keeping, dialogues, report writing, display material, communications between fictional characters and presentations to the rest of the class. The main way of working in class is through structured group work, although there are occasions for whole-class teaching as well (particularly during the introductory phases). Most of the activities described could be classed as a project and fit into a block of several weeks (for example, towards the end of a school year or after an assessment period).

The rationale
for using creative strategies

- Why do so many pupils underachieve in Key Stage 3 (S1/S2 in Scotland) MFL?

- Why do even more able pupils sometimes lose interest?

- Which contexts most help pupils learn?

- Which factors inhibit or encourage successful learning?

- How do creative strategies engage pupils in the classroom?

- Does any official documentation support the use of creative strategies?

Why do so many pupils underachieve in Key Stage 3 (S1/S2 in Scotland) MFL?

We are focusing in this book on pupils in both secondary school key stages. Most will start their foreign language learning in KS3 (S1/S2) and some begin a second MFL in KS4 (S3/S4). Some do exceptionally well but many struggle and find the subject difficult. Although many start out as enthusiastic learners of a new language, a significant number falter and begin to find they do not make as much progress as they would like. There are complex reasons for this, but one aspect of underachievement at this level may be illustrated by the following matrix:

high language high skill	**P** | **Q**	high language low skill
low language high skill	**R** | **S**	low language low skill

In the figure above 'language' represents grammar/vocabulary/text and 'high' means rich and complex whereas 'low' means simple. 'Skill' represents cognitive challenge and intellectual demand for the learner. The letters PQRS in each quadrant are used for ease of reference.

The experience of too many pupils is quadrant 'S' – an undemanding task related to language of little personal interest, for example: *Listen to a dialogue about shopping and answer a series of questions to determine comprehension of the text.* This is a useful assessment exercise but its value as a teaching activity is debatable.

Even when we take a close look at quadrant 'Q' which looks more promising (the language is more complex), the problem remains. The language may be more demanding in terms of syntax and vocabulary, but if the task is unchallenging then it will not be motivating nor engage the pupils' attention. For example: *Listen to a transactional dialogue in a hotel foyer where there is a customer wishing to book a room with various facilities for a specified number of nights* – the difficulty here is lack of perceived relevance for the learners.

If we look more closely at the task set and make it challenging intellectually, we have a greater chance of engaging the pupil with the language. This is illustrated in quadrant 'R' where there is a limited amount of language at the disposal of the pupil but where the skill area is demanding. For example, pupils are required to pick out from a dialogue in the target language selected items of vocabulary; they are not required to comprehend what is spoken but merely to write down the items that they have been allocated – times, numbers, colours, places. This can be made more or less demanding by the amount of support that the teacher offers – less support (no pauses, background noise, more items to listen for) or more support (repeated hearings, use of pause button, only a few items). In this way work can be differentiated without a great deal of extra work on the part of the teacher. Although the amount of language is small, the skill level is high.

This can even be replicated in quadrant 'P' with high language. Ask a top set pupil to listen to a sustained section of speech from a native speaker on any given topic. The pupil then has to extract grammatical items (e.g. verbs in the past tense) or strings of vocabulary (e.g. all the feminine nouns) and list them. This can be made more difficult by increasing the length of speech from 15 to 30 seconds or by adding further complexity (e.g. muffled voice).

The point here is that the difficulty of the task is increased by the difficulty of the skill level and not by making the language more complex.

Why do even more able pupils sometimes lose interest?

Professor Theo Wubbels from the University of Utrecht has identified some of the problems encountered by beginning teachers which endorse the points above and go some way to explaining why some language lessons can run out of steam:

> *Many beginning teachers struggle with class management and providing appropriate challenge for their pupils because they have too much to concentrate on all at once. The unmotivated and reluctant learners need motivating activities. So the teacher spends a good deal of time thinking up activities which will stimulate and motivate this group. The teacher makes the assumption that the motivated will study smoothly without any prompts from her.*
>
> *A stable pattern emerges – the teacher provides many activities for the unmotivated and assumes the motivated will do as they are told. The unmotivated consequently become ever more dependent upon the teacher, whereas the motivated become themselves demotivated because of benign neglect. Their initial interest is simply not reinforced.*
>
> *Both groups need sustained intellectual challenge.* (1992)

These points are also highlighted in Gary Chambers' book *Reflections on motivation* (2001) where he describes Dörnyei's motivational framework. Although developed in a context for teaching English to non-native speakers, there are nevertheless some specific aspects for MFL teachers which provide food for thought.

For example, when describing the course-specific motivational components of any learning situation, key aspects should:

- include attractive content;
- arouse and sustain curiosity and attention;
- introduce the unexpected;

- increase pupils' interest and involvement in the tasks;
- facilitate pupils' satisfaction with presentations and celebrations of success.

With teacher-specific motivational components, he highlights:

- learner autonomy;
- sharing responsibility;
- motivating feedback;
- tasks as learning opportunities to be valued;
- facilitating rather than ordering.

Finally, he stresses the importance of group work with group-specific motivational components:

- encourage discussion of the group's goals;
- promote development of group cohesion;
- use co-operative learning techniques;
- include evaluation of the group's rather than individuals' performance.

Which contexts most help pupils learn?

The twin problems of content and context are perennial ones for the MFL teacher. When language is dissected into its constituent parts for a particular lesson (grammar/vocabulary) it is necessary to put it together again for some pedagogical purpose. If the re-assembly takes place in a context devoid of significance for the learner and merely serves as a vehicle to practise the grammatical construction or recall the vocabulary, then it is easy to see how the exercise can have little intrinsic worth for a young learner. If on the other hand an authentic setting is chosen where the language is to be practised, the terminology may be either too 'rich' for the learner to comprehend fully or the cultural barriers may be too great for the learner to understand the interaction, even if he or she understands the individual words or phrases.

One of the aims of this book is to show how the very context itself (the location of the linguistic interactions) can aid the creative process and thereby aid language learning. These 'creative contexts' are locations within which linguistic input is situated and where creativity is given a chance to flourish.

The two contexts chosen to illustrate this point are, at a simple level, a village (initially represented by a grid – in effect a series of map references) and, for a more complex approach, a block of flats. These contexts derive from the concept of *simulations globales* devised by Jean-Marc Caré and Francis Debyser during the 1970s in France for the teaching for French as a foreign language. (*Simulations globales* are explained more fully in Chapter 3.) In addition to these creative contexts, Chapter 7 contains further ideas for language exploitation in a creative way which can either be incorporated into the storylines mentioned above or used on their own.

It is frequently the case that teenage learners do not like talking exclusively about **themselves** in language lessons. They are by and large interested in the outside world and have many interests in common, most noticeably:

- music;
- sport;
- fashion;
- TV;
- relationships;
- travel;
- parties.

They are also interested in some world events and concerns such as:

- environmental issues;
- health;
- future employment;
- social issues;
- peace.

They have emotional concerns (such as anxiety about performing in front of their peers and a fear of failure) and these also need to be taken into account in the MFL classroom. This affective side of the teacher–learner contract should not be underestimated. In our lesson planning we rightly spend a considerable amount of time on academic and physical issues. How will the pupils understand this point of grammar? Is this activity intellectually challenging enough? Is the room big enough for drama and can all the pupils see the teacher? Do we also spend enough time focusing on the emotional factors?

Which factors inhibit or encourage successful learning?

As Krashen (1981) has pointed out, in order for our pupils to be receptive to the comprehensible input from the teacher, they need to be free of anxiety and have a good sense of self-worth.

Stress and anxiety in the classroom can provide a barrier between teacher and pupil which effectively minimises the chances of learning taking place. What Krashen termed 'the affective filter' can have potentially serious consequences in the MFL classroom where attentiveness and engagement are crucial if the learner is to take on board what the teacher is trying to communicate. The affective filter of anxiety and low self-esteem needs to be removed so that the input can reach the learner.

Just as anxiety may inhibit learning, so success can improve learning. If pupils can achieve even moderate success at each stage of their learning, then that may in turn set up a virtuous circle of success → motivation → success. This resonates not only with the experience of teachers in the classroom, but also with a well-established psychological law. Thorndike's Law of Effect (1913) certainly has significance for us here:

> *When a response is followed by a reward (or feeling of satisfaction) the response is more likely to be repeated in similar circumstances.*

If we rephrase this in terms that we can all identify with:

> *When the efforts of a pupil to communicate in the target language are followed by a feeling of satisfaction that the message has been received and understood, then those efforts are more likely to be repeated in similar circumstances.*

How do creative strategies engage pupils in the classroom?

Many of us look enviously upon our colleagues who are able to address adult themes in their classrooms and regard with awe the Continental European pupils who discuss knowledgeably in English a variety of topics. We may want to tackle such issues with our classes but come up against the problem that our pupils simply do not have sufficient linguistic knowledge to cope in any meaningful way. This can lead to boredom for the pupils and to frustration on our part when we ask the pupils to simplify everything to the point of banality in order to extract any information at all.

The perceived need for relevance as a prerequisite for effective communication is well illustrated in the following quotation (Littlewood 1981):

> *The underlying message, then, is that foreign language teaching must be concerned with reality: with the reality of communication as it takes place outside the classroom and with the reality of learners as they exist outside and inside the classroom.*

However, as Jean-Marc Caré has pointed out so succinctly, reality for both teacher and pupils is confined within the four walls of the classroom: *'La seule réalité de la classe, c'est la classe'* (the only reality of the classroom **is** the classroom).

However hard you try to create a fiction that the class is now in some foreign location, the noise from the playground, the school bell and the exigencies of the physical environment all work against you. The pupils have to imagine that they wish to engage in some transaction, perhaps to buy some items in a shop. Leaving aside the almost universal experience of shopping in supermarkets (and therefore the lack of any meaningful communicative context), the pupil enters the shop, greets the shopkeeper, requests an item or two, ascertains the price and departs. The whole transaction may take two minutes and then the pupil is back where he or she started – in the classroom awaiting the next task from you.

This scenario, a familiar one in classrooms up and down the country, puts an enormous burden on you. You are continually having to invent new situations and contexts where pupils may interact with foreign interlocutors. Examination board specifications may also be seen as restrictive if they focus to a large extent upon consumer transactions and travel enquiries.

In attempting to create an **illusion of reality** (a term first coined by A. Maley in 1980), you may merely create an environment which is unreal, uninteresting and which does not engage the mind of the pupil. The fundamental problems with this approach are as follows:

- The pupils are essentially passive.
- The context is fixed.
- There is little room for manoeuvre.
- The task is fixed by a set phrase mentality.
- Topic vocabulary dominates to the exclusion of other useful items.
- The transactions tend to be short and have little or no sense of reality.
- The requirements of GCSE speaking tests often dictate content – although this may be useful for assessment purposes it is less helpful as a teaching device.

It is not surprising, therefore, that many pupils find such a diet uninspiring and do not continue with their study of languages beyond Key Stage 4 (S4 in Scotland).

The creative strategies (both simple and more complex) that are proposed address these issues head on. They include the notion that learning tends to be more successful when:

- it is cognitively demanding;
- both pupils and teacher are not overly stressed;
- there are elements of humour and fun;
- it is purposeful and of interest to the learner;
- resources match learning requirements.

Does any official documentation support the use of creative strategies?

There are three key official documents which underpin and endorse the creative strategies outlined in this book. They are:

- the National Curriculum Programme of Study;
- the KS3 National Strategy;
- the QCA scheme of work.

Each of them refers to the need for pupils to think about their own way of learning and be able to talk about the problems they encounter and the gains they make. The documents also stress independence on behalf of the learner, using the target language imaginatively, developing thinking skills. They are to be used as planning documents in the short, medium and long term and each leaves plenty of space for the kind of development of extended speaking and writing that we propose.

Creative strategies need to be planned into lessons on a regular basis and cannot be left to chance. Each of the above documents recognises this fact and refers on several occasions to the need to provide opportunities for pupils to use their languages in a variety of contexts and for a variety of purposes.

This documentation is concerned with teaching and learning. Even when we focus on assessment requirements, we can see that creative approaches are included in many of the aims of exam boards. There is also an example in Appendix 1 taken from the GCSE specifications from one exam board to illustrate this point.

Key extracts from the three official documents can be found in Appendix 1 on pp81–84.

key points

- High cognitive demand combined with a small amount of language can produce a significant increase in pupil engagement.

- We need creative strategies for language learning that are both intellectually stimulating and emotionally satisfying.

- The very context of the language is as important as the content in enabling pupils to participate actively in their learning.

- Success and motivation are key factors in helping pupils learn.

- Teachers can use creative strategies to help pupils learn more effectively. Such an approach can affect significantly both class management and pupil achievement.

- The need for creativity is endorsed by a number of official documents and exam board specifications.

A simple approach to creative contexts – setting the story in a village

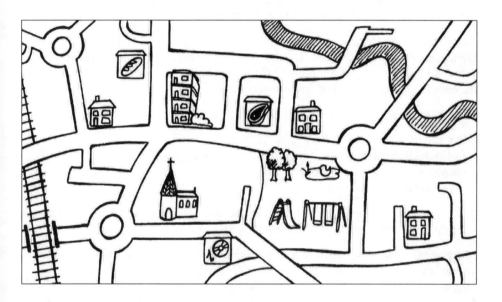

- What is a creative context?

- How much time should be
  devoted to this project?

- How do you get started
  on the project?

- Using the grid to start the story

What is a creative context?

As we have already established in the previous chapter, creative contexts are hypothetical places where people meet naturally on a day to day basis and they are located in a country where the target language is the normal means of communication. They are designed to give the maximum opportunity for pupils to use their target language actively.

The creative context in this chapter is a village, the setting for a story which the pupils themselves will create and develop. Into this village the pupils will introduce characters who will interact with various people. In this way the pupils will be able to practise a number of dialogues and role plays in an unfolding story.

The teacher first introduces the pupils to the village by means of an OHT overlay of map references. We call this the grid. The grid provides an easy tool for quick reference to a variety of locations, e.g. A6 = school / C7 = church. It also provides an opportunity at the outset to practise numbers, letters and colours.

Here are the four key points highlighted in Chapter 1 for engaging pupils:

- low language and high skill;
- intellectually challenging and emotionally satisfying;
- success orientated;
- pupils as active participants.

The purpose of the grid is to draw together the discrete strands of learning from prior learning in the classroom and synthesise them into one on-going project.

Many pupils will have learned a large amount of grammatical constructions and vocabulary on a range of topics or themes. These learned items may quickly be forgotten if not re-worked in a meaningful and active way by the pupils themselves. The focus is very much on the pupils developing a storyline by themselves with guidance from you rather than you doing all the work.

How much time should be devoted to this project?

Because of the nature of this project, it is a good idea to be able to set aside a reasonable amount of time for its completion. There are four distinct phases to the project and each will need incorporating into medium term planning arrangements.

The four phases of the project:

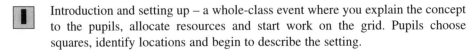

Introduction and setting up – a whole-class event where you explain the concept to the pupils, allocate resources and start work on the grid. Pupils choose squares, identify locations and begin to describe the setting.

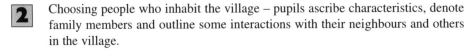

Choosing people who inhabit the village – pupils ascribe characteristics, denote family members and outline some interactions with their neighbours and others in the village.

Developing the storylines – pupils construct further conversations with other characters. There may also be some other interactions at this point, e.g. using sound effects.

 Drawing to a close. Towards the end of the project it is a good idea to find a way of drawing the whole story to a natural conclusion, for example, all the characters could go on holiday.

There are two distinct ways of incorporating this project into medium term planning, either a four- to six-week block of time at the end of term (after assessments) when all or nearly all lessons can be devoted to the project, or a six- to eight-week block where (for example) one lesson a week becomes the project lesson.

It is important to see the work on this project as an opportunity to practise previously learnt grammar and vocabulary. It is not a question of adding the project to existing coursebook or scheme of work demands, but rather an incorporation of the project as a way of rehearsing, repeating, practising and performing known material.

For example, if previous lessons have focused on topic areas such as house and home, travel and transport, pets, leisure activity, then the pupils can practise using the very vocabulary learnt in a new context. Instead of practising such vocabulary in discrete exercises, they incorporate it into a developing storyline. Thus the vocabulary becomes relevant because the pupils are using it for their own purposes and they are making choices about what they want to say or write. By actually manipulating the vocabulary and grammar in this way, pupils are also helped to memorise and understand the target language, so the work on the project provides a context where language can be practised.

How do you get started on the project?

You introduce the project initially in an unobtrusive way and arouse the pupils' curiosity by presenting the grid on the OHP. Each pupil also has his or her own blank grid. This grid is in effect the outline of a plan of a village using grid references A–H and 1–8.

The pupils suggest various grid references (e.g. A2 or C1) and you colour them in. The pupils colour in their own squares in the same way. After several squares have been filled in, you reveal to them that you are beginning to design a village and you ask for suggestions as to what each of the squares could represent. Gradually, you are setting the scene for a 'soap' which the pupils will help create. You are outlining the plan of a village and filling in details of buildings and other areas (with the grid providing a handy reference point for all locations). You then introduce the people and finally set up the interactions.

If you have recently taught the class the following vocabulary: pets/school subjects/modes of transport, then you can bring these into your questions about the village and its inhabitants. These questions can be linked to any book or scheme of work that is being used with the class. Because the pupils are creating their own reality they are more likely to be engaged in the substance and content of the work. After a while they may wish to ask some of their own questions or add extraneous detail that you may not have considered.

Ask a series of questions based on known vocabulary, and as you do so the pupils start to build up dossiers of information about the developing story. The dossiers are useful evidence of written work and may be used for formative assessment purposes. (See Chapter 6 about assessment of learning.) However, they are also useful source material for any pupil in the class when seeking to find out about a character, a particular location or the progress of a relationship.

As you introduce the separate stages of the soap based around life in the village, so the pupils build up their dossiers with appropriate vocabulary. They start with simply describing the setting, then move to the introduction of the people and finally add the dialogues and action. These dossiers could follow this pattern:

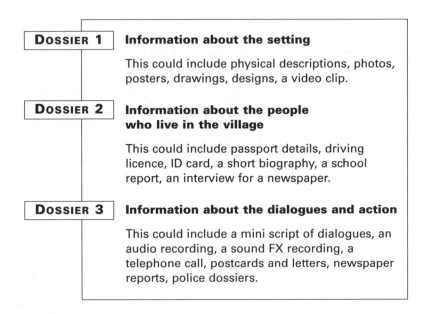

DOSSIER 1 | **Information about the setting**

This could include physical descriptions, photos, posters, drawings, designs, a video clip.

DOSSIER 2 | **Information about the people who live in the village**

This could include passport details, driving licence, ID card, a short biography, a school report, an interview for a newspaper.

DOSSIER 3 | **Information about the dialogues and action**

This could include a mini script of dialogues, an audio recording, a sound FX recording, a telephone call, postcards and letters, newspaper reports, police dossiers.

The telling of a story based around the lives of people living in a village can incorporate a large amount of the vocabulary and grammar expected of pupils in Key Stage 3 (S1/S2).

As the story develops so you can weave in previously taught vocabulary about:

• personal information;
• house and home;
• pets;
• travel and transport;

as well as grammar such as:

• prepositions;
• past/present and future tenses;
• adjectives and adverbs.

The following section shows the step by step approach to starting this project with your pupils and sustaining their interest over several weeks.

Using the grid to start the story

French and Spanish versions of this may be found in Appendix 2 on pp85–87.

Stage 1

	1	2	3	4	5	6	7	8
A								
B								
C								
D								
E								
F								
G								
H								

- Put the grid (as above) onto an OHT and place on the overhead projector.
- Provide each pupil with a blank grid (as above).
- Pupils will need coloured pens for this part of the activity.
- Each pupil will add the details to his or her own copy of the grid as the lesson progresses.
- This grid will provide the map references which will be used for describing the various locations around the village.
- You keep the master copy (the OHT) which pupils will add to later when they introduce other locations.

Stage 2

With the grid on the OHP, make the following three requests in German:

Q: *Gebt mir bitte eine Nummer.* (Please give me a number.)
A: *Zwei.* (Two.)
Q: *Gebt mir bitte einen Buchstaben.* (Please give me a letter.)
A: *A.* (A.)
Q: *Gebt mir bitte eine Farbe.* (Please give me a colour.)
A: *Rot.* (Red.)

Colour in the appropriate square with the appropriate colour (see below). The pupils then colour in their own grids in the same way.

Now invite the pupils to provide further numbers, letters and colours which you then fill in accordingly on the grid. The pupils also colour in their own grids so that they match the one on the OHP.

	1	2	3	4	5	6	7	8
A		▦						
B								
C								
D								
E								
F								
G								
H								

This can go on for as long as you like but essentially you are encouraging the pupils to provide a template or framework of coloured squares. This grid with the coloured squares is forming the map references for the village so that they can easily be referred to later on.

Stage 3

After some time of questions and answers, the grid will begin to fill up, as below.

	1	2	3	4	5	6	7	8
A		▦				▤		
B			◸		▤	▦		▦
C	▤			▤		▦		
D			▤		▦			
E	▤							
F	▦						▦	
G				◸				
H								

There are likely to be several different colours (represented here by symbols) on the grid. The colours could be direct representations of locations. Blue might be for a river or pond, green could represent a school, black could be a church, red could represent a shop, etc. After stage 3, each pupil has the same pattern on his or her grid and this resembles the OHT.

Stage 4

Das Dorf

	1	2	3	4	5	6	7	8
A		🔲				▦		
B			◢		▦	▤		🔲
C	▤			▦		🔲		
D			▦		🔲			
E		▦						
F		🔲					▤	
G					◢			
H								

At this point you add a title to the grid: *Das Dorf* (The village).

You then make the following suggestions:

▦ represents *der Fluss* (**river**);

▤ represents *die Schulen* (**schools**);

🔲 represents *die Geschäfte* (**shops**);

◢ represents *die Kirchen* (**churches**).

Then ask a series of questions to build up the context more fully:

- *Wie heißt der Fluss?* (What is the name of the river?)
- *Was für Geschäfte sind sie?* (What kind of shops are they?)
- *Ist das eine Grundschule?* (Is it a primary school?)
- *Ist das eine katholische Kirche?* (Is it a Catholic church?)

These questions can go on for as long as you feel that the class are with you and are contributing actively to the process. There are no right answers, but each answer is accepted and added to the whole picture with you making any linguistic adjustments that are deemed necessary.

Stage 5

When you have established the variety of locations on the grid, you then turn to introducing the characters who live and work in the village. Let us take just one shop as an example: A2.

- *Das ist die Bäckerei.* (That's the baker's.)

You then ask the class as a whole:

- *Wie heißt der Bäcker?* (What is the name of the baker?)
- *Hat er eine Frau?* (Has he got a wife?)
- *Wie heißt sie?* (What is her name?)
- *Haben sie Kinder?* (Have they any children?)
- *Wie viele?* (How many?)
- *Wie alt sind die Kinder?* (How old are the children?)
- *Wie heißen sie?* (What are their names?)
- *Gehen sie zur Grundschule im Dorf?* (Do they go to the primary school in the village?)
- *Wie kommen sie dahin?* (How do they get there?)

And so on ad infinitum. The questions can flow from you as guidance for the pupils. This is a real opportunity to practise using the target language actively and to cement understanding by repetition and meaning in context. The questions derive in part from the previous lessons with you and the material covered. You model the way in which questions are asked in order to elicit information and the pupils can then use these questions themselves when carrying out their own investigations later.

It is useful if another person (Foreign Language Assistant (FLA), non-teaching assistant, student teacher, sixth former, able pupil) could write up the answers on the board and so model how the information is to be recorded.

For example, answers could be modelled either in the form of a table:

Der Bäcker?	Herr Schulze.
Frau?	Er hat eine Frau.
Name?	Sie heißt Meike.
Kinder?	Sie haben Kinder.
Wie viele?	Zwei.
Wie alt sind sie?	Fünf und acht Jahre alt.
Wie heißen sie?	Thomas und Bernd.
Gehen sie zur Dorfschule?	Sie gehen zur Dorfschule.
Wie?	Zu Fuß.

or in full sentences, underlining useful grammar: *Sie gehen zu Fuß zur Schule.*

The pupils write down these answers to the questions and then later use this written evidence to build up a dossier or archive to exploit further when they are creating their own stories.

Stage 6

Das Dorf

	1	2	3	4	5	6	7	8
A	▦	▦	▥			▤	▭	
B			◢		▤	▭		▦
C	▭	▭		▤	▭	▥	▦	
D			▤			▦		
E	▦	▤					▭	▦
F		▦	▥				▭	
G			▭		◢			
H	▥	▥	▥	▥				▭

This can then lead to a further exploitation of the grid as a whole-class activity or else as a group exercise with each group embellishing the layout of the village in their own way (see above). This would also mean that the group would have to come up with an explanation of their own for the various additional categories such as:

represents ?

represents ?

represents ?

A pupil may need to ask for help with vocabulary, such as: '*Wie sagt man auf Deutsch: 'forest'?*' (How do you say 'forest' in German?)

When you have labelled sufficient squares with the number of pupils in the class, it is time for the pupils themselves to begin to apply their knowledge of the target language. It is a good idea for them to work in pairs at this point so that they can support and encourage each other.

Each pair is then allocated one square which is their own to exploit and develop. The allocation can be done by drawing lots, pupils making a choice or whichever system you prefer. Thirty-two pupils will need, therefore, sixteen squares.

It is the task of each pair to:

- describe the location;
- invent the characters who live or work there;
- begin to plan a meeting or dialogue with other characters in the village.

To begin with, each pair needs to follow the template provided in stage 5. There are examples of what is needed in terms of information in Chapter 5.

The pupils keep their information about their character in a class box file (or ring binder) which is a master set of all the characters in the village. You keep this for reference, so that you can monitor and assess written work as well as have a resource file of all the different characters in their various locations.

Stage 7

Das Dorf

	1	2	3	4	5	6	7	8
A								
B								
C								
D								
E								
F								
G								
H								

Some thoughts about working in groups or pairs:

Even at the outset it is good to train the pupils to be independent learners and to cope as far as possible within their own resources. So let us here introduce the class management technique of the inspirational Danish language teacher Leni Dam. Dam sets out three key principles when encouraging pupils to work in a relatively independent way to result in more flexibility for the teacher to deal with groups and individuals in a more productive way.

First, she encourages each pupil to seek three other sources of information before asking the teacher for help. Younger pupils are already being encouraged to do this under the National Literacy Strategy:

- They could ask a friend.
- They could look up the word in a dictionary.

• They could enlist the support of an FLA or other classroom assistant.

Second, she points out that she only has so much time at her disposal and because there are so many pupils to see she will spend just five or ten minutes with each group or pair in the classroom (depending on the size of the class and time available). She then visits each group or pair for the purpose of intervention, clarification, occasional translation and encouragement as well as further questioning about the characters that the group has invented and their various lifestyles. The pupils need to realise that the teacher's time is precious and that time you spend with each group needs careful negotiation. They also need to consider whether they are just going to ask for a series of translations or whether there could be some more useful purpose – such as a grammatical point, help with the next step of the story, guidance towards resources and so on. These are useful organisational skills in their own right.

Although there is a lot of question and answer practice in oral work, there is plenty of writing practice as well. Pupils need to note the answers to questions in order to build up individual dossiers on the characters they are inventing, details of buildings and their dimensions, evidence about the local environment, etc. The following categories are examples of what might be included in a dossier (for more ideas on what to include see Chapter 5).

Grid – H6

Location – railway station	Personality
Dimensions	Family details
Description	Pets
Near to	Favourite pastimes
Distance from other locations	Favourite sports
Some interesting features	Link to prior learning – for example, if working on 'travel and transport' then include subheadings
Inside the location	
Outside the location	
Characters who live/work there	Preferred means of transport
Name	Getting to work
Age	Going on holiday
Description	At the weekend

Third, when groups or pairs report back at a plenary she encourages them to elect a spokesperson and say 'we think' rather than 'I think'. This develops a certain amount of group solidarity, protects the less confident individuals and encourages more interactions.

Stage 8

When the pupils have completed a dossier on their location and characters, it is time for them to interact with other characters in the village. With a class of thirty-two, you will have sixteen squares allocated.

Write the squares on sixteen pieces of paper and draw them out of a bag at random. For example, if the first one out is A2 (the baker) and the second one out is H6 (the railway station), then these two pairs now form a group of four.

When all of the squares have been drawn, the pairs then re-assemble in groups of four. Each group will now have two dossiers with the information about the location and characters. Their task is to invent a dialogue between one character from each location at a meeting on one of the squares.

So the person who works at the railway station goes to the baker's and they have a conversation. The group has to compose a dialogue in the target language lasting about one to two minutes and preferably one which contains a surprise or problem at the end.

The dialogue is intended to be performed in front of the rest of the class so that they can all see how different characters respond in different situations.

The written dialogue is placed in a dossier and used by other pairs or groups for later interactions. Both spoken and written dialogues can be used for assessment purposes later on.

Stage 9

The final master grid may look something like this.

Das Dorf

The pupils have identified a large number of locations and allocated place names, buildings, open areas and houses to them.

This could be put on a large A1 poster on the classroom wall with either words or pictures indicating various locations:

	1	2	3	4	5	6	7	8
A		baker's						
B							pond	
C				school				
D						park		
E			church					
F		disco					sports stadium	
G								
H						railway station		

They have also introduced characters who live and work there and have begun to write some short dialogues between them. They have started to outline various possibilities with plots and a number of ways in which characters could interact. The pupils can also perform some of these dialogues in front of the class. They have kept their dossiers of archive material on their chosen characters as well as their dialogues (in written form as well as possibly on cassette).

key points

- The scene for a simple storyline is set by outlining a series of map references for a village on a grid.

- The teacher models how each square can become a certain location inhabited by various people.

- Pupils then take over this model and adapt it to create their own storylines.

- Particular emphasis is put upon effective working in groups or pairs.

- Pupils practise both oral and writing skills while developing the project.

- Pupils perform dialogues in front of the class. Written work can be used for formative assessment purposes.

3

A more complex approach to creative contexts

- How can we develop
  this simple approach?

- Where did the ideas for the
  more complex creative context
  come from?

- Why use the context of
  a block of flats?

- What is the role of
  the teacher in this method?

How can we develop this simple approach?

The creative context in this chapter represents a methodology combining four key elements for successful language learning. It is:

- **interactive** – pupils working with other pupils and the teacher;
- **cognitively challenging** – the intellectual demands of the project are high;
- **emotionally literate** – there is a satisfaction in creating your own story;
- **purposeful** – it utilises grammar and vocabulary in a meaningful way.

In the previous chapter we saw how you can locate a soap around the setting of a village where the pupils can create short scenarios based in fictionalised settings with guidance from you. The initial map grid references eventually become redundant as the pupils introduce more buildings and other places into the village. Once they have taken on the role of their characters they can then perform dialogues and keep a written record of events.

The level of interaction between pupils (and teacher and pupils) is likely to be relatively limited and based on the amount of vocabulary and grammar learnt in the three years of Key Stage 3 (S1/S2 in Scotland).

We now come to a more developed version of the soap which is appropriate for more advanced learners of the target language.

Pupils have learned a good deal of vocabulary and grammar in their first two or three years of language study. They now have the opportunity to apply this vocabulary and grammar in a new context. This helps with memorisation of vocabulary as well as improving understanding of the grammatical constructions. In addition, as they learn more complex forms of the language, they can add these into the developing storyline.

Where did the ideas for the more complex creative context come from?

We saw in the previous chapter how younger pupils can relate easily to the idea of characters who live and work in and around a village. Older pupils will need greater intellectual demands to sustain their interest and to give them more opportunities to practise the target language.

There are two principal sources for the idea of a more complex creative context – the setting of the story in a block of flats.

First, there is the research in the field of the **more able** and in particular the notion of **cognitive challenge**.

To aid pupils' development teachers need to ensure that tasks are sufficiently challenging and complex. The brain enjoys complex problem-solving. Simply put, if we require pupils to spend most of their time copying, then they may only become good copiers. Cognitively challenging tasks that require higher order thinking (e.g. critical or analytical) can aid linguistic development. The importance of questioning (from both teachers and pupils) should not be underestimated; the best questions arouse curiosity, awaken interest and trigger higher order thinking. 'The true value of a question is to develop learning rather than test for knowing.' (Smith and Call 2001)

Teachers need to allow pupils to take risks; getting it wrong is not failure but learning. You can promote effective learning by assisting the pupils' performance. Having completed a task, pupils need to be given opportunities to reflect not only on what they have learned but also how. Rather than just offer praise or criticism for a piece of work, you could offer further encouragement by asking: *How did you work that out? What did you mean by ...? Where did you come across that expression?*

As Vygotsky (1962) said: 'The teacher, working with the school child on a given question, explains, informs, enquires, corrects, and forces the child himself to explain.'

Pupils can be trained to become well versed in thinking skills. They need to go beyond the basic acquisition and application of existing knowledge into the realms of creative and complex thinking. These include the ability to reason, to make informed judgements and to critically evaluate information. In the classroom pupils need not only challenge but also support from you and other pupils. In essence, cognitive challenge in the classroom is well summed up by Morelock and Morrison (1996):

> *The classroom environment plays an important part in the development of thinking skills. An environment that will recognise and nurture the developing skills and accept new ideas without reservation will encourage a child to express thoughts freely, confident that new and offbeat ideas won't be met with ridicule or rejection. The child is then able to take risks and be creative.*

Second, there is the concept of *simulations globales* developed in France in the 1970s by Jean-Marc Caré and Francis Debyser as a method for teaching French as a foreign language (FLE).

Traditional role plays leave little room for manoeuvre and are fixed by the exigencies of the situation or context. They can lead to a sequence of short autonomous dialogues with little room for progression. In contrast, *simulations globales* provide a progressive construction of reality where the world is re-invented according to the disposition of the learner, with the teacher providing for assisted performance. The fundamental point about this approach is that it moves the learner from a passive role to an active one and the teacher from a source of knowledge to a collaborator in learning. *'Simulation'* here does not solely mean imitate, reproduce or do like, but invent and create. *'Globale'* means that in place of isolated role plays in contrived contexts, the whole learning experience is encompassed. For example, the pupil does not simply buy a ticket; he or she goes on a journey and has a variety of experiences, conversations and reflections.

Teachers and learners together invent a setting and place within it the characters who will act out the soap. The story has to be located in a real life context and here we have chosen a block of flats where a variety of families and individuals will interact on a daily basis. We are indebted to Debyser for this idea from *L'immeuble* (1986).

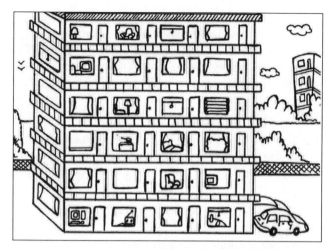

Why use the context of a block of flats?

For older pupils we move the location into a town or city and the characters into a microcosm of society – a block of flats. This context has a number of advantages:

- Characters are all located at the same address and therefore will share some experiences.
- Characters will inevitably have a number of transactions as they cross paths with other residents.
- A block of flats can offer a certain degree of anonymity.
- A block of flats throws a variety of people together who may or may not enjoy the experience of living in close proximity to their neighbours.
- It is therefore a rich source of the kind of storyline that makes soaps successful.

It is probably most helpful for teachers in the UK to locate the block of flats in the target language country (or country where the target language is the principal language). We have an enormous barrier to overcome in terms of xenophobia and fear or lack of understanding of foreigners (Convery et al 1997). By placing the context firmly in the everyday reality of the target language country the teacher will give the opportunity for stereotypes and caricatures to emerge and be confronted. The dynamics of the situation create the story of which the pupils themselves have the ownership.

This method of language teaching and learning recognises and acknowledges the problems of lack of motivation, reluctant learners and the need to provide intellectual challenge as outlined in the introduction and does not minimise the difficulty of the situation in any way. Rather, what *simulations globales* propose are creative strategies that seek to move the pupils from a state of passive acceptance of whatever is placed before them to an active role where they make choices about the content and context of the lesson.

It is well known that many pupils like stories, fantasies and computer games (e.g. *Tomb Raider, Quake, Lara Croft*) and films based on fantasy (e.g. *Star Wars, The Matrix*).

Role play games are still very popular (especially with teenage boys, e.g. *Dungeons and Dragons* and *Games Workshops*) and fantasy literature retains a wide appeal (*The Lord of the Rings, Harry Potter, The X Files*). Part of the appeal is that pupils engaged in such stories and fantasies can make choices about the outcomes. They can attribute characteristics to various people, they can invent punishments and rewards and they can simulate battles and conflict. In so doing they may well act out some of their own personal anxieties and there is a well recognised cathartic effect in many of these games.

The most popular kind of TV programme for teenagers is the soap. The reasons for the popularity of this genre of TV are many and various. However, the essential characteristics of any successful soap may give a clue as to why they remain popular. They contain:

- lots of parallel and interconnected storylines told simultaneously;
- short scenes of approximately 2–3 minutes;
- complex emotional relationships in a community;
- a mirror on reality which arises out of everyday situations;
- the same structure – introduction > climax > cliffhanger.

The central theme of all soaps is the same everywhere: relationships, and the top three contexts are family, love and friendships, with work and enemies not far behind. The themes are always topical and up-to-date and are easily addictive. As with eating fast food, everyone watches but few admit to watching too many.

Now, suppose it were possible for you to harness some of this enthusiasm, passion and intrinsic interest for fantasy and soaps and bring them all into the world of your classroom. Instead of passive pupils accepting the diet provided solely by you, they actively create their own with guidance from you. There would be the **reality of illusion** where pupils are involved dynamically in the creation of their own world and their own stories and in which they can confront some of their own personal preoccupations obliquely and yet purposefully.

Creative contexts provide a progressive construction of reality where the teacher allows pupils to create their own world. There is less emphasis on content and more on learning how to learn. Creative contexts show just how this can be achieved by harnessing the creative imaginations of the pupils to the innovative pedagogy of the teacher.

The fundamental principles of these creative contexts are:

1 Pupils need to become actively involved in the process of learning in order to learn languages effectively – this includes an awareness of their own learning skills and learning strategies.

2 Teachers need to encourage their pupils to be active and willing participants in the learning process in order to teach languages effectively – this includes an awareness of their own preferred methodology and pedagogy.

3 Pupils need to feel a sense of purpose for their classroom activity which relates to the outside world for relevance and to the inside world of the classroom for fun and intellectual challenge.

The joint enterprise whereby teachers assist the learners to learn and the learners take responsibility for their own learning (while drawing on the support and guidance of the teacher for explanation, resource management and teaching of basic structures and vocabulary) is a vision of how MFL classes could operate.

The creative contexts form a template into which existing				
schemes of work	GSCE specifications	Scottish Standard Grade	National Curriculum Programme of Study	coursebooks
		all fit.		

The practical application of the method is explained in Chapter 4. The rationale for this concept may be summarised as follows:

• The pupils are active.
• The pupils are personally engaged in the story and have ownership of it.
• There is no settled and complete context – the context is progressively created as a joint enterprise.
• There is plenty of flexibility and the process develops over several lessons.
• There is variety in both vocabulary and structures – pupils learn better what they want to know and handle personally (spoken and written).
• There are longer dialogues and descriptions.
• The pupils control the outcome of the narrative.

Current assessment requirements may not always fully engage and stretch the learners. The emphasis throughout these creative contexts is upon three clear things:

• the learner as an individual;
• a move away from a rigid adherence to a prescribed and structured pattern;
• an accent on creativity and interaction.

Every day in every MFL classroom we ask our pupils to suspend disbelief. We ask them to pretend. We ask them to imagine they wish to carry out this or that transaction. We ask them to put themselves in a foreign country for the purposes of communication.

So we start with this suspension of disbelief and take it a step further. We all learn by pretending and that is the core of the learning contract. It is a necessary part of the languages classroom. At the beginning we ask our pupils to create their own reality in the form of their own world with the characters who inhabit this world and interact. This kind of virtual reality can be much more real than some of the attempts at authenticity that we may try out in the classroom.

What is the role of the teacher in this method?

The teacher has multiple roles. At one moment you are a learning manager helping pupils choose resources, at another you are a motivator making suggestions for interactions; here you are an adviser on grammatical structures and there you are an evaluator of performance. The point is that at all times you are a highly active and directive participant in the process.

Pupils may well resist new ways of working and, despite their outward appearance, many teenagers like routine and accepted ways of doing things. As with all new approaches it is probably advisable to start with a top set with whom you already have a good rapport to give the whole enterprise a chance to work. Good working relationships are essential when trying out new strategies because they then give maximum opportunity to test the effectiveness of the strategy itself. As class management adviser Bill Rogers (2002) says: 'Co-operative learning needs to be structured and taught over time and is normally more effective when the class is **relationally cohesive**'.

There are times when certain lexical items and points of grammar need some introduction, exemplification, explanation and modelling by you. For example, prepositions and adjectival agreement can feature during the setting up of the location or tenses during some of the interaction. However, rather than being discrete points which have no relevance to the task in hand, they can be integrated into the whole so that they have a particular relevance and context.

Using this method will include the establishment of pairs and groups and in some cases individuals. Your principal role is to provide the necessary stimulus to the pupils to set the soap in motion, to guide them towards appropriate resources, to offer advice upon organisation of the dossiers and to help with vocabulary and grammar when it comes to writing dialogues.

key points

- After the first years of language study in secondary school pupils are ready to deal with more complex projects.

- One of the main sources for this approach is the research into teaching the more able and the need for cognitive challenge in language teaching.

- *Simulations globales* provide an opportunity for meaningful speaking and writing through extended creative role play.

- Pupils are engaged in a developing storyline of their own creation and are thereby encouraged to take risks with their language learning.

- Teachers have a facilitative role in the classroom and thereby encourage their pupils to be more active as language learners.

Setting the story
in a block of flats

- How do I introduce
  this project to the pupils?

- How should I organise
  groups for this project?

- Are there any specific
  class management issues
  around group work?

- What kind of outcomes can we
  expect from pupils?

- What kinds of written exercises
  work well with this project?

- How can I integrate grammar
  into this project?

How do I introduce this project to the pupils?

- Put a representational outline of a block of flats on the OHP.

- Provide each pupil with such an outline of a block of flats.

4				
3				
2				
1				

- Now set out the context, telling pupils in the appropriate target language that in a city of 300,000 there is a block of flats, and that you would like them now to choose a floor in the block of flats on the outline. Choose one of the floors in your block of flats on the OHP and colour it in. Now choose one flat out of the several on that floor.

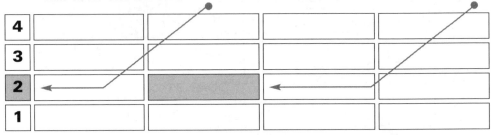

Pause at this point and consider what resources you will need to help with the creation of this soap. Ask the pupils what resources they think you will need to help them to create a story based in a block of flats in the target language. Here are some suggestions:

- dictionaries;
- Internet – to find occupations, addresses, useful information about towns;
- coursebook – to refer to previously learned vocabulary/look up grammar points;
- catalogues – ideas for decorating the flat/dressing people;
- phone books – names, addresses, phone numbers;
- newspapers – useful plot ideas;
- magazines – photos of famous people/colourful locations/horoscopes.

How should I organise groups for this project?

Once the pupils have chosen their individual flats, move them on to working in pairs or groups of four. In this way they can start to explore the language required and create their first dialogues. It is a good idea, therefore, to spend some time planning the organisation of these pairs and groups.

When asking pupils to work in groups, we need to be sure that they are working **as** a group, each pupil being clear about his or her role and how to interact with other group members. As Diamond (1998) has said: 'In the classroom we should teach children how to think for themselves. One way is to group children so that they're talking to one another, they're asking questions of one another, they're learning to be teachers.'

Pupils can be involved in selecting the criteria for the formation of groups:

- Choose partners you like.
- Choose partners you work well with.
- Choose partners you think you can learn from.
- Choose someone you have seldom or never worked with before.
- Choose partners who would like to work on the same activity as you.

Be prepared for some initial confusion or uncertainty. The whole class needs to identify difficulties and issues so that effective ways of organising collaborative working can be agreed.

- Have 'positive' rules on each table, e.g. *Listen to the contribution of each member of the group and value what they have to offer.*
- Ask pupils to choose roles (chair, writer, reporter, resource gatherer, etc); these can be rotated.
- Organise the names in advance and not more than four.
- Allow some pupils to write on their own.
- During a presentation phase ensure all pupils participate so that there is a common purpose.

The serious purpose of the whole enterprise needs to be clearly understood by the pupils and the parameters of group work carefully explained and in some cases negotiated.

The dynamics of group work need to be carefully considered. At the beginning of some projects there can be intense enthusiasm from pupils and this can lead to some discouragement later if the expectations are unrealistic or if they do not work according to established ground rules. Similarly, some pupils may not take the project seriously – if it becomes over-funny or too fantastic, the class clown can take over and the whole thing degenerate. This is where your skills as planner, negotiator and facilitator are paramount. This is theatre, not therapy. Although not a psychodrama, there may be some emotions aroused by the context, characters or interactions. Pupils need to change roles from time to time so that they do not become fixated or bored with just one character. Each group can provide something permanent to be kept in an archive or dossier. Each contribution needs to be valued and conserved so that the pupils feel the whole activity is worthwhile.

The ideal group would contain:

- someone reasonably good at the target language and able to take the lead;
- a good artist;
- someone with good ICT skills;
- a good actor.

The interaction between such a group could be extremely purposeful, creative and rewarding. The whole in the group can be greater than the sum of the parts as long as each member contributes and feels that his or her contribution is valued.

Are there any specific class management issues around group work?

There may well be some class management issues when using such creative strategies for the first time and these points may help:

- Avoid stupidity, clichés, dull stereotypes and the grotesque.
- Written work can be drafted and re-drafted (preferably word-processed if at all possible so that it can be easily corrected and look good on display), monitored by you and assessed where appropriate.
- Photographs and pictures can add to the colour.
- From time to time, there should be a presentation (drama, display) with each group showing their best contribution.
- Occasional use of video and/or cassette recordings can enhance the performance.

Quality does not mean perfection. It means each pupil giving of his or her best to the group in a collective task and thereby improving their knowledge of the target language. Such tasks are primarily for performance (to enhance speaking skills, confidence and self-esteem) and display (to enhance writing skills and accuracy).

What is the next step?

The first thing the pupils need to do is describe their flat and its surroundings in more detail. You can tell them that if this was a soap on TV, we would need to know all about the local environment so that we would have a sense of community and be able to relate to the characters.

To begin with, the pupils need to describe:

- the number of rooms in the flat;
- the furnishings;
- household equipment.

They can re-use vocabulary learnt at an earlier stage. Because they are creating their own fictional location, there is more incentive to use this vocabulary than when they are using it for a stand-alone coursebook exercise. This categorisation of vocabulary is an important feature of the early work on the project. Not only will the pupils need nouns and adjectives but also prepositions, verbs and adverbs. This active use of vocabulary in building physical descriptions gives pupils an opportunity to use their prior language learning in a new context.

The pupils write out their descriptions of the different flats and keep them in a dossier or archive. Keep this dossier in a central location so that pupils can have access to it when working on dialogues in a later session. You can assess this work after the group has carried out a self-correction (especially valuable using word-processing). Oral presentations can be marked in terms of fluency, accuracy, pronunciation, communication. Written work can be marked either as a group project or individual item.

How do the pupils describe the surroundings?

This stage gives many possibilities for introducing aspects of cultural awareness.

For the country where the block of flats is located, encourage the pupils to avoid clichés and introduce countries other than Spain/France/Germany – why not Latin America/DOM-TOM/Austria/Switzerland? The target language country is of average size and has a wide variety of inhabitants. It is up to each group or pair to decide if the block of flats is in a large city, capital or medium sized town.

Groups now need to locate their block of flats in a specific town or city. It needs to have an address and for this they will need the name of the block of flats, number, street name, town and postcode. This is where a few town plans can be useful reference materials – encourage the pupils to move beyond the familiar and well worn.

For example, if they come across:

see if they can add something a little different such as:

In France there are many streets named after famous people – the pupils could invent their own according to their favourites:

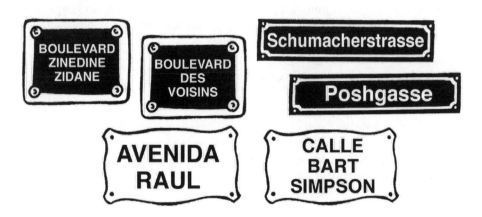

The layout of the address itself is an important cultural reference point and fulfils National Curriculum requirements in an inventive way.

Now let us turn to the outside of the block of flats:

What notice could there be on the front door?

What kind of writing might be found on the outside walls?

Graffiti often appears on the walls of blocks of flats. What kind of graffiti could each group write in the following categories?: something personal, something political, something poetic, something simple, a witty saying, a proverb, advice to the reader, something bitter-sweet.

What kind of places would we find in a community?

Street corners invariably have shops on them. Next door to the block of flats is a shop or row of shops. The group must decide what kind of shop it is, bearing in mind its proximity to the flats. Here are some examples of shops they may find:

French

boulangerie, pharmacie, boucherie, coiffeur, traiteur

German

Bäckerei, Metzgerei, Supermarkt, Buchhandlung, Lebensmittelgeschäft

Spanish

panadería, carnicería, farmacia, bodega, tienda de ultramarinos

They then need to give a name to the shop (name of person/colour/feature).

It is a particular time of year (Christmas/summer holidays/local festival). What can one see in the shop window? And the prices (in euros of course!). What adverts are on the window? What small postcards are stuck on the door? Pupils keep all the information in their dossier and they can use it later for a poster advertising the shop and/or town.

Is there a garden or small park attached to the block of flats? Some groups could add a description of the garden or park to their dossier and use it as a location for a particular encounter.

What kind of vehicles are kept at the block of flats?

Give the pupils the following scenario:

The block of flats has some garages attached. Each family/flat is entitled to one garage. What kind of vehicle does each have or which of the following vehicles belongs to which family/person? Each group has to ascribe a vehicle to their character (if they have no vehicle then they need to offer an alternative form of transport).

Describe each vehicle (or the special one for the family): new or second-hand? How many miles done? In-car entertainment? Pupils could invent one extra type of entertainment or gadget for their car, e.g. back seat entertainment controls.

You could give the following dilemma to some of the more able pupils:

• There are only so many garage spaces and too many flats – who gets no garage? What criteria would you draw up to help with this decision?

How do we introduce the main characters into the location?

Now that the location has been established we move on to the introduction of the principal players who will take part in this soap.

Model a dialogue based on the following suggestions, with a helper who takes the role of a new character who has recently moved into the flats. Ask the questions in the target language. The helper replies in the target language and writes the answers up on the board. This is the beginning of the dossier that each group will keep on the characters.

How long have you lived here?	Private life – friends and loves.
Date and place of birth (think beyond the target language country).	Principal events in his/her life – success and failure/luck/bad luck/trips abroad.
Do you have any particular leisure activities?	Present occupation
Brief biography – school/university or first job/favourite sport.	

Each group now concentrates on choosing a character (or characters) and ascribing details to them. This could be done for some invented purpose such as police files, a census return, marketing exercise. Descriptions should include the following detail:

Sex	Clothing	Habits – *every Thursday they play cards, go shopping with their friend, drink champagne*
Title (Mr/Mrs/Miss/Dr)	Accessories	
Physique	How they walk – *with a stick, a limp, slowly, whistling, with a dog on a lead*	Profession
Face/eyes/hair/skin colour		Overall impression
Appearance		

What would an initial dialogue between neighbours sound like?

Let us imagine that two new neighbours have met on the stairs and need to introduce themselves to each other.

N1	Hello.
N2	*Hello.*
N1	How are you?
N2	*I'm fine – and you?*
N1	I'm fine. May I introduce myself? I am …
N2	*And I am …*
N1	I am new to this area.
N2	*Where are you from?*
N1	I'm from (name of large town).
N2	*Oh, I have an uncle who lives there, etc.*
N1	Can you tell me anything about this place?
N2	*Well, let's see. What would you like to know?*
N1	What are the neighbours like?
N2	*Well, …*

This could continue for as long as the pupils like. Encourage them to use vocabulary and structures with which they are familiar from previous language learning. They can ask each other all kinds of personal details, e.g. recent holidays, the weather, latest sports results, as well as information about the flats, travel arrangements locally, good shops in the neighbourhood and so on.

What kind of outcomes can we expect from pupils?

At different points during this project, we need to take stock of what the pupils are achieving and use that monitoring process in their formative assessment. There is more about assessment in Chapter 6, but at this point let us look at some of the learning outcomes we can expect from the pupils after the first seven stages of the project.

Oral – each of these could be recorded for assessment purposes:	*Written – each of these could be used for assessment purposes:*
• a simple description of their flat and its surroundings (in the style of a news reporter giving background to a story); • an introduction to their principal character (in the style of a dating agency video); • a dialogue between two neighbours meeting for the first time; • a dialogue between two characters meeting by chance or by arrangement; • an explanation of the criteria for who has not got a garage (in the style of a game show); • a cassette recording of a phone conversation with a friend describing the location of the flat.	• a written description of the flat (in the style of a police burglary report); • a written description of the principal character(s) (in the style of an awards ceremony); • the dialogues above (in the style of a radio soap episode); • the criteria for who has not got a garage (in the style of a school report); • adverts and small classified ads on postcards (in the style of TV shopping); • a poster publicising the local shop (in the style of a promotional campaign); • PowerPoint presentation of an estate agent selling a flat.

What kinds of written exercises work well with this project?

Writing frames are a useful way of helping pupils to organise their thoughts into coherent and articulate sentences. There are two excellent exercises using writing frames in the CILT publication *Just write!* (Adams and Panter 2001) which fit in very well with the style of this project.

WHY USE WRITING FRAMES?

Writing frames help pupils to become 'writers' in the foreign language, rather than just labellers of pictures or copiers of text. Increasingly in the National Curriculum there has been a move towards developing explicit skills in language learning and use of language. Frames contribute towards this by developing writing skills and showing how texts are constructed. Pupils joining Year 7 will be familiar with the use of writing frames from their work in Key Stage 2 and will also encounter them in other curriculum subjects in Key Stage 3.

GAMES USING A WRITING FRAME

The structured approach to writing presented in a writing frame lends itself well to writing games and group writing activities.

Carousels 1

Make a photocopy of the blank writing frame for each group. Each group writes a section of the frame (in order), then passes it on, for the next group to complete the following box. Each group ultimately does the same amount of writing, but doing this as a game adds variety.

Carousels 2

Cut the writing frame into separate sections; each group then completes one section. Reassemble the sections afterwards to see if the complete text makes sense.

Carousels 3

Each group adds to the content of each section already completed by previous groups, e.g. the first group writes: '*Je m'appelle Madonna*'. The second group adds: '*Mon nom de famille est ...*'

Consequences

This game is much the same as Carousel 1 described above, except that the teacher writes the name of the 'subject' at the bottom of the writing frame; each group fills in one section and folds it over, securing it with a paperclip, before passing it on to next group.

Mad Libs

Prepare a text with key words missing in each box of the writing frame. Number the spaces of these words. Make a list of the missing words by grammatical category. Distribute the list to pupils and ask them to predict what the missing word might be, e.g. 1. noun; 2. adjective (do not show them the frame at this point). Once pupils have written their suggestions, reveal the writing frame, and read aloud the resulting 'gap-fill'. They will probably be bizarre, but that is the point of 'Mad Libs®'! (For more details, see any of the 'Mad Libs®' books by Roger Price and Leonard Stern, or play a game on-line by doing an Internet search for 'Mad Libs'.)

from *Pathfinder 40: Just write!* by Adams and Panter (CILT 2001)

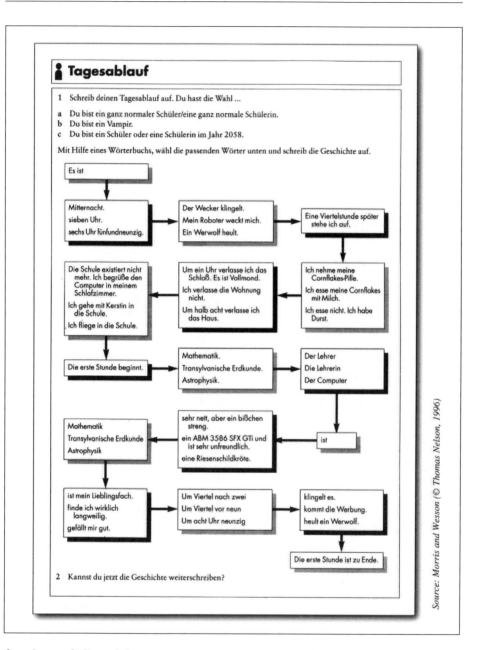

🛉 Tagesablauf

1 Schreib deinen Tagesablauf auf. Du hast die Wahl ...

a Du bist ein ganz normaler Schüler/eine ganz normale Schülerin.
b Du bist ein Vampir.
c Du bist ein Schüler oder eine Schülerin im Jahr 2058.

Mit Hilfe eines Wörterbuchs, wähl die passenden Wörter unten und schreib die Geschichte auf.

> **Es ist**
>
> Mitternacht.
> sieben Uhr.
> sechs Uhr fünfundneunzig.
>
> Der Wecker klingelt.
> Mein Roboter weckt mich.
> Ein Werwolf heult.
>
> Eine Viertelstunde später stehe ich auf.
>
> Die Schule existiert nicht mehr. Ich begrüße den Computer in meinem Schlafzimmer.
> Ich gehe mit Kerstin in die Schule.
> Ich fliege in die Schule.
>
> Um ein Uhr verlasse ich das Schloß. Es ist Vollmond.
> Ich verlasse die Wohnung nicht.
> Um halb acht verlasse ich das Haus.
>
> Ich nehme meine Cornflakes-Pille.
> Ich esse meine Cornflakes mit Milch.
> Ich esse nicht. Ich habe Durst.
>
> Die erste Stunde beginnt.
>
> Mathematik.
> Transylvanische Erdkunde.
> Astrophysik.
>
> Der Lehrer
> Die Lehrerin
> Der Computer
>
> Mathematik
> Transylvanische Erdkunde
> Astrophysik
>
> sehr nett, aber ein bißchen streng.
> ein ABM 3586 SFX GTi und ist sehr unfreundlich.
> eine Riesenschildkröte.
>
> ist
>
> ist mein Lieblingsfach.
> finde ich wirklich langweilig.
> gefällt mir gut.
>
> Um Viertel nach zwei
> Um Viertel vor neun
> Um acht Uhr neunzig
>
> klingelt es.
> kommt die Werbung.
> heult ein Werwolf.
>
> Die erste Stunde ist zu Ende.

2 Kannst du jetzt die Geschichte weiterschreiben?

Source: Morris and Wesson (© Thomas Nelson, 1996)

from *Lernpunkt Deutsch 1*

In addition to these writing tasks there are a number of exercises involving the writing of letters and postcards that pupils can do. These are still required in GCSE specifications and so are useful exam practice in their own right.

The difference we propose here is that when writing the letters or postcards the pupils could try to hide a secret message in the text for the benefit only of the recipient. This extra constraint makes the task more challenging and intellectually demanding and adds a different dimension to their language learning.

For example, one neighbour secretly declares his or her passion for another by sending a postcard with a hidden message (every fourth letter is a previously arranged code):

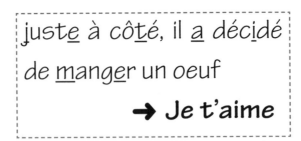

If they also write to each other, some of the letters or e-mails can describe the day's events and include a secret message as well.

Some may even want to send a text message and here they would not need to send it in code! Can your pupils find out the common French, German or Spanish abbreviations?

How can I integrate grammar into this project?

One way of introducing specific grammatical constructions into the project is to set up particular situations that you want your pupils to concentrate on and then provide a selection of grammar that they need to introduce into the dialogues.

Tell the pupils that all their characters need to be back in their flats. We now know where everyone is and this gives a measure of control as well as uniformity as to what happens next.

Choose one of the scenarios below (a snapshot of life) and tell the groups the time:

1   It is seven o'clock on Tuesday evening.
2   It is nine o'clock on Saturday evening.
3   It is Sunday morning.
4   It is breakfast time on Monday.
5   It is New Year's Eve.

Ask the pupils the following question:

What are the inhabitants of the block of flats doing at this time?

They need to devise a dialogue or a short story or brief written report and it must include a selection of the following grammatical constructions. Let the pupils decide which constructions to use. You give them the option of choosing a minimum of three from the list:

- Subject + verb: *P dort/P arbeitet/P duerme;*

- Subject + *être en train de* + infin.: *M est en train de se laver les cheveux;*
  Subject + *ist beim* + infin.: *M ist beim Kochen;*
  Subject + *en vías de* + infin.: *M está en vías de trabajar;*

- Subject + verb + complement: *K fait la cuisine/de la gymnastique;*
  K liest ein Buch/treibt Leichtathletik;
  K prepara la comida/está leyendo un tebeo;

- Subject + verb + time;

- Subject + verb + time + place;

- Subject + verb + time + place + manner.

Now that we know what the inhabitants are doing at this time, what are they saying while engaged in this activity and who are they talking to?

Here are a few options for the characters:

- on the phone/mobile/Internet chat line/texting;
- on the stairs/in the kitchen/in the garage.

Here is fuller treatment of another scenario along the same lines:

Where was she and what was she doing on 30 July?

A police officer calls and wants to know the answers to the following questions about Mme X (this could be the character herself or a report about her character):

The group then writes up the report, using the answers as a basis for the writing, from the point of view of the police officer.

1	Where was she on 30 July?	7	Was she carrying anything
2	What was she doing?		unusual?
3	What was she wearing?	8	Did she take her car?
4	When did she go out?	9	If so, describe the car.
5	Who with?	10	If not, did she go on foot or by any
6	Did she return – and if so was she		other form of transport?
	alone?	11	Did she seem anxious?

They could write a postcard or letter from Mme X to her mother about the events of that day using the constructions given above.

How can smells be used for creative writing or expressing an opinion?

Tell the groups to put all their characters back in the flats because it is now midday.

Around lunchtime in France, Germany or Spain (and other countries where these languages are spoken) you can often get an idea of just what people are having for lunch according to various smells wafting out into the street. Many recognise the Proustian power of smell to evoke memories, affections, loathings or just good cooking.

Where are all these smells coming from? From which flat do they emanate?

Pupils are given the following suggestions of smells (or can even smell some of them!) and have to ascribe them to various flats. They then have to give a reason for their choice:

I think I can smell paint. Mr Z lives in number 45 and he is decorating his kitchen.

Strong	Peculiar	Paint	Flowers
Garlic	Coffee	Petrol	Rotten eggs
Light	Vomit	Gas	Barbecue
Beer	Alcohol	Sweat	Burning
Nauseating	Cigarette	Perfume	Baking

What opportunities are there for extended writing/speaking with sound effects?

Here is another technique that can be very successful in building up suspense, awakening imagination and encouraging the pupils to make innovative use of their subject knowledge.

First of all, announce to the class that all the families and characters have to be back in their flats. This is a good way of re-establishing order and keeping everything in perspective. With all the people back on home base, announce to the class that it is now three o'clock on Sunday morning. They are about to hear a number of noises and each of their characters has to react to the sounds they hear.

You could model the reaction of one of the characters by inventing a dialogue between him or her and someone else in the flat. If the person lives alone he or she could phone (or text) someone and tell them about what he or she hears.

Play the sound FX on CD (for easier and more precise sounds) or cassette. A good sequence would be:

- loud footsteps;
- pause and knock at door;
- door opening noisily;
- further footsteps – possibly running;
- a scream …
- silence.

Pupils could either:

(a) write a short descriptive piece outlining what happened (in the style of a tabloid news report) or
(b) make up a short telephone conversation with one character telling the story and the other offering question prompts as follows:

- How do the characters react?
- Describe what they heard.
- Questions from the other person – ask for repetition/clarification.
- And then what happened?
- What did you do next?
- Did you phone the police? Why/why not? And so on …

(NB Sound FX CDs can be purchased at any large music store and are a worthwhile investment for any departmental budget.)

After following the pattern you have established the pupils can then have a go themselves in devising their own sound FX episodes and recording them onto cassettes to play in front of the class to accompany their description of events.

key points

- A block of flats is chosen for the soap because that is where a variety of people will interact on a natural and regular basis.

- The soap is created by the pupils according to storylines of their own choosing.

- The pupils first devise the setting, then they invent the characters and finally the interactions between the characters.

- There are plenty of opportunities for extended writing and grammar practice within the project.

Using resources creatively
to support the creative contexts

- What information
  is required about each character
  in the village or block of flats?

- What are the best questions for
  eliciting information?

- What resources and materials
  will I need in the classroom?

- Which grammatical structures
  most naturally fit
  this introductory section?

This chapter provides a wealth of ideas and resources for you to guide the pupils in building up the scenarios in the village and the block of flats.

What information is required about each character in the village or block of flats?

Introduction – when introducing each character, the following information may be added to each dossier. This then will form a crucial database for the class when planning further interactions and plot developments with the characters.

> - Names*
> - Ages
> - Family
> - Professions/jobs
> - Nationality
> - Make of car
> - Physical description
>
> - Favourite clothes
> - Characteristics
> - Likes/dislikes
> - Favourite activities
> - Friendships
> - Unusual pastimes
> - Pets

* When allocating names to their characters, some pupils can easily find family names in the telephone book but struggle with finding first names. This is where the Internet comes in handy. The lists of first names in Appendix 3 were found very quickly by typing in 'first names France' (or Germany or Spain) in the search engine **www.google.com**.

What are the best questions for eliciting information?

The framing of any question by the teacher is crucial, as is your response to the pupil's replies. Each of the following questions is just a starting point, a springboard for further information. The answer in itself is not important – it is the way in which the answer will suggest other possibilities and further development that is critical. **The pupil's response provides the teacher's next question.**

Here is a sequence of questions that you might want to ask to help the pupils with their first character dossier:

- What is the family name?
- How old is the central character?
- How many family members are there?
- What is his/her profession/job?
- Has he/she got a car and if so, what make?
- What nationality is he/she?
- What is he/she like?
- What clothes does he/she prefer?
- What does he/she like/dislike?

- What does he/she like doing in his/her leisure time?
- Who is his/her best friend?
- Name one unusual activity he/she does.
- Has he/she a pet?

Here is an example in French of how this can develop:

Qu'est-ce qu'il/elle aime faire?   *Il/Elle aime jouer au foot.*
Avec qui?   *Avec ses amis.*
Quand?   *Samedi.*
Tous les samedis?   *Oui, tous les samedis.*
Et à quelle heure?   *A trois heures.*
Où jouent-ils?   *Au stade.*
C'est au centre-ville?

and so on ad infinitum. It is important during this line of questioning for the pupil (or one of the group) to make a written note of the answers so that a dossier of information can be built up.

What resources and materials will I need in the classroom?

The following resources are likely to be useful when undertaking one of the projects or creative strategies. The list is not exhaustive, nor is it probable that classrooms would contain all these items. However, the greater the choice of resources for the pupils to access, then the greater the possibility of their independent learning:

- telephone book from each country for names
- clothing catalogue
- furniture catalogue
- department store catalogue
- jobs – use yellow pages from the Internet: **wfa.pagesjaunes.fr/pj.cgi**
  www.gelbeseiten.de
  www.paginasamarillas.es/home
- classified ads from other countries
- car adverts
- sports/fitness clubs adverts
- pet shop information
- FLA and other native speaker adults
- list of useful websites
- dictionaries – both monolingual and bilingual
- rhyming dictionaries (such as *Rimes* by Larousse) (for graffiti)
- magazines and newspapers (e.g. *Authentik* material)
- computer with Internet access.

The following checklist is a useful *aide-mémoire* and can be photocopied and kept on your desk.

What resources and materials will I need?

Have I prepared suitable questions to get started on the project?

Are all these resources to hand?

- ☐ cassette recorder/CD player
- ☐ flashcards/visuals
- ☐ pens/paper/scissors
- ☐ dictionaries
- ☐ catalogues
- ☐ coursebooks
- ☐ computer room booked/stand alone computer
- ☐ videos/TV

Have I organised groups appropriately?

- ☐ number per group
- ☐ mixed ability
- ☐ group leaders identified
- ☐ ground rules established and understood

Have the tasks been negotiated with each group?

- ☐ dialogue (taped/performed/written)
- ☐ playlet
- ☐ report/account
- ☐ story/poem/song
- ☐ website/page(s)
- ☐ PowerPoint presentation
- ☐ poster

Have I allocated sufficient time for each part of the lesson?

- ☐ have clear focus for introduction (e.g. grammar point)
- ☐ set time limits for group task and give reminders
- ☐ encourage learning to learn (teacher is last resort)
- ☐ allow short time for clearing up

Do the pupils know what will be assessed?

- ☐ a particular grammar point, e.g. the ability to use the past tense
- ☐ the overall accuracy of a piece of work
- ☐ a specific language skill, e.g. speaking fluently

Are there any opportunities for teacher assessment?

- ☐ allocate set time to spend with each group
- ☐ circulate to monitor and identify good learning/misconceptions
- ☐ share learning/clear up misconceptions with whole class in plenary
- ☐ establish pupil self-evaluation through learning logs
- ☐ allow time for group to agree next steps

Which grammatical structures most naturally fit this introductory section?

Not only do we want the pupils to create attractive and imaginative stories, but we also want them to speak and write accurately and with a good grasp of grammar.

Right from the outset of working on either the village project or the soap based on the block of flats, we can integrate grammar practice into question and answer sessions that the pupils can then re-use in their dialogues.

Here is an example in French of revising the following grammatical point in a short dialogue:

> **colours / comparisons / superlatives / like + verb / to be / to have**

Teacher with one group discussing characteristics of inhabitant of the village:

M. Lebrun, est-il grand ou petit?
Il est grand.
Est-ce qu'il est plus grand que Mme Lebrun?
Oui.
Qui est plus grand – lui ou elle?
Il est plus grand.
Est-ce qu'il n'est pas aussi grand que Pierre?
Non.
Et Jean-Marc?
Il est plus grand que Jean-Marc/Il n'est pas aussi grand que Jean-Marc ...

key points

- Guided questions from the teacher are a vital part of helping the pupils develop the project along constructive lines.

- The more authentic source material you have in the classroom, the more easily pupils will be able to access it for crucial parts of the project.

- The Internet is a most valuable resource for information on a variety of issues for the project.

- Key grammatical structures can be incorporated into both the spoken and written parts of the project.

Exploiting the contexts

- What does a worked example look like?

- How would you follow up a dialogue between two people?

- How does this approach fit in with the exam board specifications?

- How can you assess pupils' work?

- How can pupils assess themselves?

What does a worked example look like?

After the pupils have established the locations and their surroundings and invented the characters that they want to inhabit their flat, the soap begins to take on a life of its own.

If we take the block of flats as the main context, then we already know that many families and different people live there. We now want to bring these characters together so that conversations may arise naturally and minor provocations develop, reflecting real life.

At this point pupils need to brainstorm ideas to suggest a list of occasions when and where the inhabitants of the block of flats might meet during any particular day, for example:

- children meeting in the play area;
- a meeting with other tenants to make a complaint;
- an interview with a local minor celebrity;
- an encounter on the stairs with an animal/someone carrying a ladder/the postman;
- a discovery in the lift of an unwelcome stranger/a large item of furniture/an unpleasant smell.

Each encounter will inevitably lead to a conversation of some sort. These conversations can follow the well-trodden path of any GCSE/Standard Grade role play initially, but the context allows for more fruitful continuation on the part of the pupils. For example, at Key Stage 4/S3 or S4 French it could look like this:

Monsieur Dupont is a reporter on the local daily paper. He has just discovered that one of his neighbours in the block of flats is Jean-Claude Rosbif, a footballer on the local team and so he arranges to interview him as a feature in the paper.

M. Dupont:	*Jean-Claude, je vous remercie beaucoup pour cette interview aujourd'hui.*
Jean-Claude:	*De rien.*
M. Dupont:	*Vous jouez pour Marseille depuis combien de temps?*
Jean-Claude:	*Deux ans.*
M. Dupont:	*Est-ce que vous aimez bien jouer pour cette équipe?*
Jean-Claude:	*Oui, bien sûr. Mais je voudrais bien jouer pour Lens.*
M. Dupont:	*Pourquoi Lens?*
Jean-Claude:	*Parce que je suis né à Lens.*
M. Dupont:	*Quelle est la date de votre anniversaire?*
Jean-Claude:	*Voyons voir ... c'est le ... le neuf mars.*
M. Dupont:	*Les jours de match, que mangez-vous normalement?*
Jean-Claude:	*Je mange des pâtes, du riz, de la purée, et quelquefois de la viande, du poisson.*
M. Dupont:	*Que faites-vous le matin des matchs à domicile?*
Jean-Claude:	*Je me lève très tard, je me lève vers 10h00 du matin, et puis je prends un bon petit déjeuner ... et ben ... je me rends au stade.*
M. Dupont:	*Pratiquez-vous un autre sport que le foot?*
Jean-Claude:	*Je pratique le golf.*
M. Dupont:	*Merci bien pour l'interview, Jean-Claude. Au revoir.*
Jean-Claude:	*Je vous remercie, aussi. Au revoir.*

The conversation can revolve around the vocabulary taught in connection with any context or area of study – in this case sport and leisure. The protagonists simply have to use the vocabulary in their dialogue to bring it to life in an active way.

How would you follow up a dialogue between two people?

A follow-up for a future lesson or for homework could take the following forms:

- conversation between M. Dupont and his wife about the interview (narrative in the past tense). *Ce matin j'ai interviewé Jean-Claude Rosbif et il m'a expliqué que ...;*
- postcard or e-mail sent by M. Dupont to his brother recounting the interview (written exercise using past tense);
- postcard or letter sent by Jean-Claude to his mother telling her to buy the paper because his photo and interview are in it (written exercise using past tense);
- poster for the forthcoming football match;
- small ad for football kit;
- newspaper article about the recent poor form of the local team;
- M. Dupont's interview in the paper;
- radio or TV recording of the interview.

Of course, the follow-up needs to be tailored to the type of dialogue conducted – these ideas can easily be adapted.

How does this approach fit in with the exam board specifications?

The creative contexts provide the framework in which the apparently worthy but almost unattainable objectives of the exam board specifications may be reached because it is the pupils themselves who provide the impetus and imperative for action. It is the dynamics of the situation that create the story of which the pupils have the ownership. Guided by the teacher, they create, invent, develop and embellish their own narrative. The GCSE specification gives full justification for such an approach (and indeed endorses it in many places).

The extract shown right, taken from a GCSE specification (Higher Tier), illustrates clearly how the creative contexts can provide useful practice before exams:

Candidates will be expected (...) to:
- cope with a degree of unpredictability;
- deal with a widening range of potential problems;
- use and understand a widening range of vocabulary and structures, including some unfamiliar language;
- discuss issues and give opinions;
- give full descriptions and accounts.

How can you assess pupils' work?

The strategies presented in the preceding chapters offer many opportunities for pupils to be actively engaged in their own learning, working independently of the teacher in pairs or groups and exercising a degree of choice over what they wish to produce. Ideally, they will be motivated to say or write what **they** want on topics of personal interest.

Collaborating with others to produce, for example, mini dramas or recorded conversations, pupils will be taking risks and their work will almost certainly contain more errors and reveal any number of misconceptions. However, we do not want to demotivate them by grading their work or placing too much emphasis on marks.

Let's consider the worked example from p56. From an initial conversation between M. Dupont and Jean-Claude, pupils could subsequently produce a conversation between M. Dupont and his wife about the interview, write a postcard from Jean-Claude to his mother telling her to buy the newspaper or record the interview and present it as a news item.

In the following example pupils have decided to interview Jean-Claude about his daily routine. The teacher has been focusing on the present tense, including the use of reflexive verbs, and is looking for accurate work. The pupils have had access to a dictionary.

> P   *Jean-Claude, tu te lèves à quelle heure dans le matin?*
> J-C *Les jours du match à neuf heures et demi.*
> P   *Que mangez-vous normalement?*
> J-C *Au petit déjeuner je ne mange rien. Je prende du café. A midi je mange avec tout l'équipe. On mange du riz ou des pâtes.*
> P   *Que fais-tu après le match?*
> J-C *Normalement je rentre chez moi et je regarde la télé. De temps en temps je vais au restaurant avec ma femme.*
> P   *Et, tu te couches à quelle heure?*
> J-C *Je me couche à onze heures.*
> P   *Merci Jean-Claude. Au revoir.*

How can we assess this to improve pupils' learning? School policy may require teachers to grade work or allocate a numerical mark, but grades and marks alone do not tell pupils how to improve the standard or quality of their work. In providing comments to pupils rather than mere marks we can focus on improving their learning. They need to know what they have done well and be given explicit guidance on what they must pay attention to next. Allocating marks (half a mark deducted for accents or agreements and a full mark for a spelling mistake) may actually demotivate learners.

> *Those given feedback as marks are likely to see it as a way of comparing themselves with others (ego-involvement), those given only comments see it as helping them to improve (task-involvement): the latter group out-performs the former.* (Butler 1987: 474–482)

Before handing this work in, pupils should be encouraged to check the piece for accuracy by referring to the grammar section in the coursebook. Assuming the conversation has been produced from memory, you will want to praise pupils for creating an original piece that makes sense and contains a lot of accurate language. You might highlight other errors (e.g. *'je prende'*) and ask the pupils to correct it or, if this is a recurring error, you may choose to share the point with the whole class. The piece of work would then be re-drafted prior to presentation. The teacher's role is to question the pupils and challenge their thinking to discover how they reached particular decisions.

T   *Je prende.* Tell me how you arrived at this?

The pupils explain their thinking, prompted by the teacher's judicious questioning.

T   So, the infinitive is *'prendre'* and the first person ends in *'e'*? I want you to check this in the coursebook and note the first person ending.

T   I've also highlighted *'demi'* and *'tout'*. These are adjectives. What do you know about adjectives?

The pupils will hopefully refer to agreement in gender and number.

T   Overall, what you have written makes complete sense and is generally accurate. Make a note in your logbook about what you have learned and what you will try and do better next time.

The dialogue between pupils and a teacher should be thoughtful, reflective, focused to evoke and explore understanding, and conducted so that all pupils have an opportunity to think and to express their ideas. (Black and Wiliam 1998)

How can pupils assess themselves?

Firstly, if pupils are to self-assess they need clear and attainable learning goals and an understanding of what the finished piece of work will look like. If we want pupils to write a conversation between two people who meet on the stairs, then we will be more likely to secure success if they have had access to accurate models of the same.

Successful learners are able to reflect on their learning, acknowledging what they have done well and setting targets for improvement. The research of Professors Black and Wiliam (1998) identified pupil self-assessment as one of five key factors in using assessment to improve learning. Pupils should therefore be encouraged to keep a record of their learning.

The following is an example of a learning log. The pupil has reflected on his experience and identified new learning. Furthermore, he shows awareness of strategies that are likely to produce good results (e.g. 'We worked well as a group but only after we had agreed what to do and who would do it') and what he needs to do next to improve the standard of his work.

Learning Log – Brian Harmer   Date: 17/03/03

This week's task: *to write a conversation between two families who meet in a park*

What we did:
- *agreed a storyline and brainstormed the language*
- *made a list of words and expressions we would need*
- *Peter found the new language for us*
- *Peter and Tanya put the script on to PowerPoint for a class presentation*
- *we also recorded the script on cassette*

What I learned:
- *I know more about the perfect tense than the others*
- *I learned some new vocab and expressions (Tu plaisantes?)*
- *I'm still slower than the others with the dictionary*
- *we worked well as a group but only after we had agreed what to do and who would do it*
- *not to rely too much on the teacher*
- *we did well because we had collected everything we needed*

What I found difficult:
- *the teacher was not always available to help*
- *including questions in our dialogue*
- *using PowerPoint*

Next steps:
- *we need to redraft the script (me and Yasmin)*
- *Peter will check the PP presentation with the teacher*
- *I must get better at using the dictionary*

Pupils can only achieve a learning goal if they understand that goal and can assess what they need to do to reach it. (Sadler 1989: 119–144)

We know that expert learners are aware of a range of possible strategies to problem solve. When reviewing learning with the class, we need to provide opportunities to discuss learning strategies and allow pupils to discover what works for them. For example, we routinely ask pupils to learn new vocabulary but do we, once tested, ask them to explain or demonstrate *how* they learned the words?

key points

- Dialogues between inhabitants of the block of flats provide useful practice of a variety of vocabulary and grammatical constructions. There are a number of opportunities for writing which can naturally follow dialogues.

- Pupils need to be active participants in the assessment process.

- Much of the developing storyline links to Higher Tier GCSE/ Standard Grade specifications.

Further
creative strategies

- Are there any other ways of using creative strategies?

- What form can playful creativity take in the languages classroom?

- How can I encourage my reluctant pupils to practise speaking in class?

- How can we use nonsense words to help explain grammatical concepts?

- How can I help my pupils enjoy reading in the target language ?

- How can a dictionary aid creative learning skills?

- How can I teach listening skills more effectively and creatively?

- How can I teach reading skills more effectively and creatively?

Are there any other ways of using creative strategies?

The creative contexts introduced in Chapters 2 and 4 represent settings where pupils can devise stories around characters of their own making. They are located in a village or in a block of flats depending on the age and language competence of the pupils. However, there are other creative strategies, featured in this chapter, that can be explored in the classroom, which can either be incorporated into the telling of stories or used as free-standing methods to enhance learning.

What is the role of humour and play?

Humour is a serious business in the languages classroom. Every situation encountered gives an opportunity for a pragmatic and linguistic response by the teacher. Take, for example, the telling of jokes in French:

> **Q: De quelle couleur sont les petits pois?**
>
> **A: Les petits poissons rouges.**

The pupils may or may not laugh. Either way the silly story is a springboard to further linguistic exploration. Why is it funny? Why is it not funny? What stylistic or grammatical rule is being broken for this joke to work? Are there any other jokes that work with confusion of sounds? Do they work better in one language than another? Can you think of any similar jokes in German or Spanish?

One of the reasons why creativity is so important in the MFL classroom is that it makes work pleasant and this is not an easy task. It certainly does not mean doing anything just for the sake of it or to fill in time. It needs to be fully integrated into any scheme of work, syllabus, or work plan. Creative language learning has a lot to do with playing with words and playing on words. The learning comes through the playing. As is illustrated by the following quotation about children learning science in the early years of primary school, learning grammar may need many attempts before it is fully understood:

> *When learning is at the most fundamental level (...) don't rush! When the mind is evolving the abstractions which will lead to physical comprehension, all of us must cross the line between ignorance and insight many times before we truly understand.* (Prof D Hawkins in Holt 1967: 144)

A useful analogy at this point is the well-known building toy LEGO. Observe any children playing with it. They sort pieces. They rummage around. They pick up and discard. They make choices. Occasionally they force pieces to match. They gradually create buildings, animals, people. Often what is created does not become apparent until after much experimentation. The very process of playing with the bricks is educational in its own right. What is the child learning? Spatial awareness. Colour and shape. Collaborative play. Texture and congruence.

How can our pupils become LEGO language learners? They play with words and they play on words. They may search and sort, skim and scan, pick out and categorise the words they find. They may choose this word and that word and discard the rest. They may select words that rhyme, cognates, words with only five letters. After much sorting and selecting, scanning and choosing, they may end up with a useful selection of words and phrases which they can then use to construct some sentences. Much may not become clear until they have finished their selections. But the active playing with words is itself an integral part of the learning process and if it is left out, the learning can be fragmentary and fragile.

What form can playful creativity take in the languages classroom?

Creativity depends to a large extent upon some form of constraint. Compare these two questions:

- *What did you do at the weekend?*
- *What did you do at the weekend?* – and each sentence in your answer must contain an adverb.

The teacher provides a specific linguistic constraint (i.e. *use an adverb in your answer*) and pupils are thereby constrained to produce utterances in spoken or written form which demonstrate their understanding. These utterances may be in the form of dialogues to support one of the contexts mentioned in previous chapters. They may be in the form of a play on words which reveal a new way of looking at language. They may be funny, irritating, witty, novel – but the understanding comes with and through the playing.

With the constraint provided by the teacher the pupils experiment with words. For example the constraint may be: *Only use words of four letters.* Out of this genuine difficulty the pupils must manufacture meaningful sentences. Here are some examples in French:

Tout sera pâle, gris *tout sera trop long* *aube, soir, jour, mois* *faim, soif, rêve noir* G. Pérec	**TOUT** **ABUS** **SERA** **PUNI** seen on Paris *métro*

Of course, this is a clever device and may well be beyond the competence of most pupils. The point, however, is not to focus upon the examples but on the process itself. This is indeed the approach of the whole book. You need to adapt the examples and find your own constraints to introduce into your teaching.

How can I encourage my reluctant pupils to practise speaking in class?

Pupils are often reluctant to speak in class simply because they feel they do not have sufficient vocabulary to say what they want to say. They also fear that they might dry up and be embarrassed. How can the idea of creative constraints help these pupils?

Here is a classic constraint that works well with all ages and in all situations. It is called the **3–2–1 game** and it might be a good idea to practise it with colleagues before trying it out in the classroom.

The 3–2–1 game

Ask for three volunteers. The three then have to enact a short role play which you will provide. The role play deals with the very late arrival home of a teenager from a party. The two others play the part of the angry parents. This is an exercise all teenagers can recognise and respond to immediately!

The particular constraint is that the father may only use one word of the target language (**no more, no fewer**); the mother only two words and the teenager only three words. They should also be encouraged not to repeat any words and to hold as natural a conversation as possible.

The trio then enact the scene in front of the class. It is amazing how difficult this is to do. The language level is very low (only a few words after all) but the intellectual challenge is very high and this is what brings about a creative solution. This illustrates very well the point made in Chapter 1 about low language and high skill. This can be followed up with a written transcription of the scene which can then be recorded on cassette (even including accompanying sound effects).

Here is an example of how the dialogue might progress:

Teenager:	Sorry, late again!
Mum:	You're sorry!
Dad:	Sorry!
Mum:	Really, Tom!
Teenager:	Not my fault!
Dad:	What!
Teenager:	It was Mary.
Mum:	Mary who?
Dad:	Mary!
Teenager:	Not telling you.
Mum:	You will!
Teenager:	No, I won't ... and so on.

Pupils could spend some time in groups of three devising their mini dramas and then compete to see who can come up with the longest sustainable conversation. They could also think up new encounters which lend themselves to this kind of exchange, e.g. complaining in a shop/choosing a holiday destination/deciding what to eat in a restaurant.

See Appendix 4 pp89–90 for suggestions for the **3–2–1 game** in German, French and Spanish. These words can be put on posters around the room and used as prompts for the pupils – and they can add further ones when they get stuck. FLAs and other native speakers can be a real help in finding just the right short phrase for tricky situations.

Here is another example, taken from German. A driver is stopped by a traffic police officer and a dialogue ensues which may only take the form of questions. As soon as a question is answered the dialogue is broken.

> **Wie heissen Sie, bitte?** (What is your name please?)
> *Warum wollen Sie das wissen?* (Why do you want to know that?)
> **Darf ich die Fragen stellen?** (May I ask the questions?)
> *Wieso denn?* (What for?)
> **Werden Sie meine erste Frage beantworten?** (Will you answer my first question?)
> *Muss ich eine Antwort geben?* (Must I answer that?)
> **Wo wohnen Sie denn?** (So, where do you live?)   and so on.

Who can make the conversation the longest?

How can we use nonsense words to help explain grammatical concepts?

Grammatical concepts are notoriously difficult to explain satisfactorily to pupils.

> *Practical experience also shows that direct teaching of concepts is impossible and fruitless. A teacher who tries to do this usually accomplishes nothing but empty verbalism, a parrot-like repetition of words by the child, simulating knowledge of the corresponding concepts but actually covering up a vacuum.* (Vygotsky 1962)

However, using nonsense words can sometimes be a way of helping pupils to understand grammatical concepts without a lengthy explanation. The aim is to get the pupils to play with and use the nonsense words in a variety of contexts before asking them to see connections and links. Only after they have played with the nonsense words and discovered patterns do you introduce them to similar concepts in the target language.

For example, provide your Key Stage 3 (S1/S2 in Scotland) pupils with the following group of nonsense words. As a starter activity, invite them to categorise the words in as many different combinations as they can within a given time limit of five minutes:

bleeb	splim	meepily	krut	yoll	squirzy
grum	flenk	snidge	treb	zenk	numdle
jimble	corm	flut	modge	gandle	skrudge
stum	herry	tronn	quonky	hunj	himpily

They could categorise them (for example):

- alphabetically;
- words beginning with fl/tr;

- words ending in -ble/-eb;
- five-letter words.

Nonsense words help pupils appreciate patterns, sounds, links, suffixes and prefixes (grammatical concepts) before confronting the real words in the target language.

When they have done this first categorisation, ask the pupils to re-categorise them according to these patterns that you have invented for the words. Can they group other words underneath?

squirzy	bleeb	numdle	himpily
Adj	**Noun**	**Infinitive**	**Adverb**

What deductions do the pupils make from this exercise?

For example, they may deduce:

- words ending in -y are adjectives;
- words ending in -ily are adverbs;
- words ending in -le are infinitives   and so on.

Test this hypothesis with a range of nonsense words until it breaks down (the exception tests the rule).

If the pupils have grasped the concept of the grammatical construction, then try out the same exercise with a text in the target language. What patterns do the pupils notice (if any)? What do they deduce? When they have grasped the FORM of the word, they may well be ready to move on to the meaning and communicative possibilities. This is a session well suited to a plenary.

How can I help my pupils enjoy reading in the target language ?

This exercise is designed to help pupils into a text by focusing first upon the form of the language as a stepping stone into its meaning. The example is with a French text and is suitable for Year 7 or Year 8 (P7 or S1 in Scotland).

Provide the text below for each pupil.

Le jour de ma grande visite à Paris

En janvier je suis allé de Leeds à Paris. Je suis parti à huit heures en train de Leeds à Londres. Je suis allé avec mon copain Guillaume qui a un kangourou vert. Moi, j'ai un kangourou aussi qui s'appelle Kiki, mais il est malade et il est resté à la maison. En route j'ai mangé deux sandwichs au jambon, une pomme blanche et quatre morceaux de chocolat. J'ai bu trois verres de vin bleu et sept grandes tasses de thé. Mon copain a un frère qui s'appelle Henri et il a seize ans. Il va aussi à l'école et il aime tous les sports.

Il aime surtout le football et la chasse aux éléphants. Henri a un petit éléphant à la maison.

Je suis arrivé à Londres à dix heures et demie et à la gare j'ai mangé une banane noire et douze petits pois. Puis je suis allé à onze heures avec mon copain à une autre gare où nous avons pris le train pour Douvres. A la gare il y a un cinéma, un restaurant et une piscine. Dans la piscine il y a un grand poisson rouge qui s'appelle Yves. Il aime bien manger les tomates jaunes, les croissants et naturellement les petits chats gris. A Douvres je suis allé voir mon professeur de français, Monsieur Alphonse Vantage. Mais il n'était pas à la maison et je suis allé en bateau avec Guillaume à Calais.

2 Tell the pupils that you are going to read the text out loud in French at normal speed and then when you stop reading they should call out the next word in the text.

En janvier je suis allé de Leeds à Paris. Je suis parti à huit heures en ...

3 Then begin reading again from the start of the text and read a little faster and repeat the exercise, only this time stopping at a different word.

4 Begin reading again from the start of the text, only this time read every other word only (underlined in the text below):

En janvier je suis allé de Leeds à Paris. Je suis parti à huit heures en train de Leeds à Londres ...

Wait until a pupil calls out the correct word *'Londres'*. If no-one does, then repeat the sequence from the beginning without any explanation. It is important to leave the pupils to discern the pattern for themselves.

5 Begin reading again from the start of the text, only this time read every FOURTH word only (underlined in the text below):

En janvier je suis allé de Leeds à Paris. Je suis parti à huit heures en train de Leeds à Londres. Je suis allé avec mon copain Guillaume qui a un kangourou vert.

This time the correct word is *'qui'*.

6 When someone has spotted the pattern and said *'qui'*, move on swiftly to reading out **only the colours** in sequence. Once again, the pupils have to tell you the next colour in sequence when you stop reading:

*En janvier je suis allé de Leeds à Paris. Je suis parti à huit heures en train de Leeds à Londres. Je suis allé avec mon copain Guillaume qui a un kangourou **vert**. Moi, j'ai un kangourou aussi qui s'appelle Kiki, mais il est malade et il est resté à la maison. En route j'ai mangé deux sandwichs au jambon, une pomme **blanche** et quatre morceaux de chocolat. J'ai bu trois verres de vin **bleu** et sept grandes tasses de thé. Mon copain a un frère qui s'appelle Henri et il a seize ans. Il va aussi à l'école et il aime tous les sports. Il aime surtout le football et la chasse aux éléphants. Henri a un petit éléphant à la maison. (STOP)*

*Je suis arrivé à Londres à dix heures et demie et à la gare j'ai mangé une banane **NOIRE** et douze petits pois ...*

'*Noire*' is the answer.

 When someone has spotted the pattern and said '*noire*', move on swiftly to reading out **only the numbers** in sequence. Once again, the pupils have to tell you the next number in sequence when you stop reading.

*En janvier je suis allé de Leeds à Paris. Je suis parti à **huit** heures en train de Leeds à Londres. Je suis allé avec mon copain Guillaume qui a **un** kangourou vert. Moi, j'ai **un** kangourou aussi qui s'appelle Kiki, mais il est malade et il est resté à la maison. En route j'ai mangé **deux** sandwichs au jambon, **une** (stop) pomme blanche et QUATRE morceaux de chocolat.*

'*Quatre*' is the answer.

You can continue in this vein for as long as you like and the pupils are with you. Other ways of reading include:

- reading backwards;
- reading the first word only vertically of each line;
- reading only buildings;
- reading only names of people.

Each time it is likely that different pupils will spot the pattern. All they are required to do is call out the correct word. If no-one calls out then repeat the exercise. As soon as it is spotted, move on to the next pattern. It is a good idea to use a highlighter pen to indicate the words you read out each time.

After you have exhausted a number of patterns and words, the pupils will be very familiar with the text (particularly the first paragraph). All you have done is read it several times out loud. In order to test how well they can now recall the text, tell them to turn it over and you re-read it from the beginning at normal speed. When you stop, ask them to provide the next word. Most will be able to do it verbatim.

Speed reading is a good illustration of the **playing with** and **playing on** words method. By focusing on the skill of listening for certain cues and not on the meaning of the text, the pupils unwittingly make connections and absorb patterns. When they are familiar with the vocabulary in the text, then they are ready to question its meaning.

Rather like a magician with his patter, we want the pupils to focus on one hand and listen to the patter whilst the trick is delivered with the other hand, without the pupils even being aware of it. This form of misdirection is a good technique for enabling the learning of vocabulary.

How can a dictionary aid creative learning skills?

A bilingual dictionary can be of real benefit when practising creative learning strategies and learning vocabulary and grammar. It is a valuable tool in that it empowers pupils to make their own connections, seek their own meanings and find out about their own needs. It is a genuine learning resource because learners can make independent judgements about what they are looking for and they will find more than they are seeking. It is a mine of information and an instructional aid which, with guidance, can also be used to teach forms, meanings and spellings. Let us also acknowledge that a dictionary can also be a source of fun in that odd expressions, unusual spellings, familiar friends and quirky words can enliven our learning in unexpected ways. A dictionary can also come in handy in helping pupils form their own mnemonics for memorising target language vocabulary.

On p71 there is an exercise designed mainly for teaching French at Key Stage 3 (S1/S2 in Scotland). It can be adapted for any other language as the principle is constant. The exercise is designed to show pupils that a knowledge of suffixes and their gender pattern is a useful aid to memory when learning French. After recognising gender patterns through noun endings, encourage pupils to make up their own mnemonics to help them memorise vocabulary. This active approach to taking control of their own learning:

• aids autonomy;
• uses creativity to aid learning;
• encourages independence;
• provides intellectual challenge.

This process can be applied to grammatical rules in any language. First model the problem, then provide a solution and then invite the pupils to devise their own pattern or memory aid. The more they work on this themselves, the greater the ownership and the greater the likelihood that they will retain the grammar and vocabulary.

How can I teach listening skills more effectively and creatively?

Many pupils react negatively whenever they are asked to listen to the target language on a cassette. This is probably due to the fact that they feel that they are being **tested** on their **knowledge** of the language rather than making gains in learning. Quite often their experience revolves around listening to a text (usually a dialogue) and then answering a series of prepared questions on what they have heard. In this way they are being asked to focus on the **content** of the text rather than the **form** of the **language** itself. So here is an idea to try out next time your pupils listen to an audio recording.

First, awaken expectation and anticipation of the subject matter of the audio recording. In this instance two teenagers are discussing holiday plans. Give the pupils a few minutes in pairs to come up with as many words in French that they think that they will hear when they listen to the dialogue. After a few minutes, ask for suggestions of what they expect to hear and note these in their linguistic categories on the OHP or board. If they are suggesting lots of nouns (which is quite common), ask if anyone can suggest a verb or adjective or adverb. You could also feed in a few examples yourself if the pupils get stuck.

This exercise is about training the eye to use a dictionary and classify nouns.

1 Show pupils on an OHT the following list of French nouns ending in *-age:*

page	*garage*
rage	*âge*
bagages	*cottage*
voyage	*bricolage*
espionnage	*nettoyage*

2 Ask the pupils to:

i) categorise in alphabetical order;

ii) indicate whether they think the noun is masculine or feminine and share their ideas with a partner;

iii) test their hypothesis afterwards by finding the words in a dictionary.

In a plenary session, invite the pupils to make any observations they like about this list of words.

- Do they notice any patterns?
- Are there any surprises?
- How many are feminine/masculine?

3 Now ask the pupils in pairs to list ten nouns in English ending in *-age.*

4 They should then look them up in the dictionary and note the French + gender and write them down.

5 Ask them to re-sort this list into patterns of their own choosing.

It is important to focus on the process of categorising before the outcome, i.e. What are the criteria for the patterns? What is the reasoning of the pupils for various categories? How many of the French words in this list look like their English equivalents?

6 Ask the pupils to look again at the first list of words in French which ended in *-age.*

Would they find it useful to know how many nouns in French which end in *-age* are feminine? (Answer: six). Therefore, with this knowledge it makes it easier to use words ending in *-age* because apart from those six, **all the rest are masculine**.

7 There is a useful mnemonic which helps us remember which six they are:

*Regardez **l'image** sur cette* ***page:***

*Un lion plein de **rage** échappé de sa **cage** sur la **plage** s'enfuit à la **nage**.*

8 Repeat steps 1–6 with French nouns ending in *-ion,* only this time pupils devise their own mnemonic to aid recall of the rule.

In this way the pupils are actively contributing to the lesson and the words they suggest can be used later in a mixed-skill activity (writing about what they have heard). When you have enough suggestions on the board (about 25–30 words), tell the pupils that you are going to play the recording once and they have to note down any words from the board that they hear. If it is one of the words they suggested themselves then they can put a tick by it. At the end of the recording see who has the most ticks.

Now say that they are going to listen to the recording again and you want each of them to do a slightly different activity. The important thing to stress is that you want them to listen to the vocabulary first and not worry too much about the meaning of the text. You will work on that later.

Select from the text five or six **categories** of language that you want your pupils to listen out for, for example: colours, numbers, names, particular verb forms, words following a particular sequence (e.g. 'what is the next word you hear after the phrase *on peut ...?*).

Give these categories out to different groups in the class and ask them to note down when they hear those words. This is a useful differentiation exercise in its own right.

Play the recording and watch the pupils as they write down the words they have heard. Their body language alone will tell you if they have coped with the task. Pupils who have heard the words they have been asked to listen out for will immediately write them down; those who are less sure will not be writing anything and this will tell you whether you need to repeat the exercise.

When the cassette recording has finished, invite the pupils to feed back each of the categories of vocabulary and write them on the board under the separate headings. If they have not managed to hear all of the vocabulary, then repeat the exercise, only this time give different pupils different items to listen for. Repeat until all of the vocabulary has been written down by the pupils. Then ask them to point out any patterns they notice (for example, spellings, endings of verbs, adjectival agreements).

With all the vocabulary on the board grouped under different categories, provide the pupils with a model sentence using some of the vocabulary. Ask them to continue to create some more of their own sentences by selecting different items of vocabulary to fit into the structure provided. This mixed-skill task (using listening to promote writing) helps reinforce the vocabulary in the pupils' minds. It also gives an opportunity for differentiation by simply adding or subtracting extra items to each sentence (for example, make the sentence negative, change the subject from singular to plural).

For example, this may have been the recording you wanted the pupils to work on:

Transcript A

Françoise: *Si on allait passer quelques jours en Alsace?*

Claude: *En Alsace? Qu'est-ce qu'on peut faire là-bas?*

Françoise: *Tu n'as pas écouté l'émission à la radio hier soir? Il paraît que c'est une région très intéressante.*

Claude: *Ah bon. Qu'est-ce qu'il y a à faire?*

Françoise: *On peut visiter des châteaux, on peut suivre la route du vin, on peut voir des singes en liberté. Il y a des villes intéressantes, comme par exemple Strasbourg et Colmar. Il y a beaucoup de choses à faire.*

Claude: *Je veux bien aller à Strasbourg.*

Françoise: *Et il paraît qu'aux mois de septembre et octobre, c'est très beau.*

(*from* Tricolore – Stage 3 Teacher's Book)

Here is the list of six categories you asked the pupils to listen out for:

on peut + ...	c'est + ...	months	il y a + ...	places	il paraît que + ...
faire	une région	septembre	à faire	Alsace	c'est une région
voir	très beau	octobre	des villes	Strasbourg	aux mois
visiter			beaucoup de choses	Colmar	
suivre					

For the purposes of differentiation, give more able pupils categories such as months or places (because they have to understand the text and recognise the vocabulary to do this exercise). Although the example above contained easy to recognise months, they could easily have been *août* or *juin*. Give other pupils the 'trigger cues' (*on peut ...* or *c'est ...*) because all they have to do is listen out for the trigger word and write down the **next word or words** that they hear.

A model sentence based on the above could be:

• *On peut visiter Alsace en septembre* or
• *On peut voir des villes en octobre.*

Following the above exercise, provide every pupil with the transcript (**Transcript A**) of the text. Rewind the cassette to the beginning and ask the pupils to follow the transcript as they **listen** to the target language. Tell them that after a short while you will turn down the sound but they must continue to read along at the same speed as they think the cassette would run. Then press 'pause' and say '**Stop**!' The pupils must then underline the very next word that they think they will hear when you start the cassette playing again. At this point turn up the sound whilst the pause button is down. They then compare with their partners around them and feed back which word they think they will next hear. You write these suggestions on the board. Then tell them to listen while you release the pause button. No one will make a sound ... and you have taught your class to listen! It never fails. When they have heard the correct answer, they will want to do this exercise several times.

During these listening exercises, the pupils have been concentrating on the language – the sounds and forms of the words. They will be very familiar with the text and so if you want them now to focus on the meaning, ask them to prepare some questions for a listening comprehension exercise. If the pupils themselves process the test as a teacher would, then they are more likely to understand the text than if you do all the work for them. They can also prepare a mark scheme and you could try out some of their suggestions either with the same or a parallel group.

How can I teach reading skills more effectively and creatively?

Many pupils are discouraged from reading comprehension as such because they feel that they are being tested on language before they are taught it. Here is an idea to encourage pupils to take more responsibility for their own reading and derive some enjoyment from the learning opportunity provided.

Ask pupils to choose their own text from a coursebook or magazine or newspaper. They then have to prepare ten comprehension questions on that text for another class of pupils. In order to do this they will need to read the text and look up unknown words in the dictionary. They can do this in pairs and the questions can be in English or in the target language depending on their ability. By processing language in this way they are effectively being asked to take on the role of the teacher and this active approach to learning is more likely to aid vocabulary learning and text comprehension than if you only present pre-digested material to the class.

In order to prepare comprehension questions (like a teacher) the pupils have to read and understand the text. Once they have devised the questions (with guidance from the teacher and the key questions such as who?, what?, when?, where? and how?) they need to create a mark scheme with answers before other pupils attempt the exercise. This could be done as a homework. This exercise helps the pupils think about what makes a good question (a discussion topic in itself) and also helps those pupils preparing for public exams to anticipate the kinds of questions an examiner is likely to ask. The worksheet is provided on the next page.

key points

- Humour is a key element in the development of creative strategies in the classroom.

- Playing with words and playing on words are important ways of helping pupils to learn more effectively.

- Even nonsense words can help with grammatical explanation.

- Dictionaries are a crucial tool in the languages classroom and can help pupils with their independent learning strategies.

- Both listening and reading skills can be enhanced by a variety of creative strategies.

creative reading strategy

1 Select one text from the newspaper.

2 Prepare your reasons for choosing this text (in the target language).

3 Compare with others in the group the reasons for your choice.

4 Prepare ten questions (in English) to check on general comprehension of the text.

5 Exchange these questions with another member of the group and work on their questions.

6 Construct ten questions in the target language on the text.
(e.g. in French: *quand? qui? où? à quelle heure? comment? pourquoi?*) (when? who? where? at what time? how? why?)

7 Each pupil then evaluates these questions set by the others:

• How well did they extract the information required?
• Were they closed, specific or open questions?
• What makes a good question?

8 Pupils then devise a mark scheme for both the English and target language questions.

9 Pupils then mark the work according to their mark scheme.

'It is crucial that we leave the learners alone to grapple with the text because it is in the grappling that they discover its meaning – not if we digest it all for them.'
(Graham 1997)

Conclusion

In this book we set out to demonstrate that in order to give teachers greater professional independence and pupils greater success, there needs to be a shift towards a more creative methodology in teaching languages in school. Key aspects of this creative methodology would be:

- cognitive challenge;
- thinking skills;
- creative contexts;
- engagement of learners;
- independent learning strategies.

There is a well-known saying in neuro-linguistic programming (NLP):

> **If you always do what you've always done**
> **You'll always get what you've always got.**

The main point behind this book is that if pupils discover that what they are offered in the languages classroom is a process that they find unpalatable and restrictive rather than one that is energising and liberating, then we may well find that we continue to lose them after GCSE (and possibly even earlier). Therefore:

- We need to build on the success of the National Literacy Strategy (especially in the development of vocabulary and reading skills) that helped colleagues in primary schools.
- We need to accept the spirit of the National Strategy for Key Stage 3 (especially in relation to the development of thinking skills) and focus on teaching that inspires and engages the learners.
- We need to see that creativity has a place in the MFL curriculum as the starting point and sometimes as the very core of learning.

We believe that if pupils are offered an opportunity to display their language skills in challenging and creative situations, then they are more likely to engage with the language and be successful.

If they are given the opportunity to perform in the target language in front of their peers, to create fictional characters and to design their destinies, to write entertaining and imaginative pieces which reflect their own thoughts, then they have the opportunity to become successful and purposeful learners.

Learning is ultimately the responsibility of the learner and the creative approach described in this book does endorse concepts of autonomous learning as outlined by Page (1992) and Little (2000). Little writes (about children in a foreign country learning English in an autonomous way):

> *(...) the meanings they are encouraged to express come from within themselves; they are not those that a textbook writer believes beginners in English should be introduced to. (...) Writing plays a central role in the*

process. (...) Learners can construct their own meanings 'off-line' and then use their written texts as prompts for speaking activities.

He also goes on to say that this does require a reappraisal of methodology:

If the teacher decides to dispense with a textbook, she must construct the ongoing learning dialogue in negotiation with her learners. But then, that is the very essence of a pedagogy designed to foster the development of learner autonomy. Any textbook is a potential obstacle to the development of learner autonomy because it presents a ready-made learning dialogue in which the most that is required of learners is that they speak someone else's lines.

The relatively recent research into ways of learning (Gardner 1993; de Bono 1994; Skehan 1998) has revealed that pupils do have a tendency towards visual, auditory or kinesthetic learning styles. We have shown in this book that all three of these styles can be catered for by working in the target language in both the simple and creative contexts. There is an opportunity for drama, role playing, imaginative writing, response to stimuli, active memorisation techniques and much more besides.

In the otherwise fairly daunting tome *The Common European Framework of Reference for Language Learning and Teaching* there is a delightful reference to the 'ludic' aspect of some language learning. We need to recapture that playful quality of language learning so that learners enjoy their learning and teachers enjoy their teaching.

REFERENCES

Adams, J. and Panter, S. (2001) *Just write!* CILT.

Atkinson, T. (2002) *WWW/The Internet.* CILT.

Black, D. and Wiliam, D. (1998) *Inside the black box.* King's College, London.

de Bono, E. (1994) *Parallel thinking.* Penguin.

Brown, K. (2000) in: Green, S. (ed) *New Perspectives on Teaching and Learning Modern Languages.* Multilingual Matters.

Butler, R. (1987) 'Task-involving and ego-involving properties of evaluation: effects of different feedback conditions on motivational perceptions, interest and performance'. *Journal of Educational Psychology,* 79 (4), 474–482.

Caré, J-M. (1997) *Simulations globales.* Sèvres: CIEP.

Caré, J-M. (1999) 'Simulations globales et productions romanesques' in *Le français dans le monde: recherches et applications.* Paris: Hachette.

Chambers, G. (2001) *Reflections on motivation.* CILT.

Cheater, C. and Farren, A. (2001) *The literacy link.* CILT.

Convery, A. et al (1997) *Pupils' perceptions of Europe.* Cassell.

Council for Cultural Co-operation Education Committee, Modern Languages Division, Strasbourg (2001) *Common European Framework of Reference for Languages.* CUP.

Dam, L. (1995) *From theory to classroom practice.* Authentik.

Debyser, F. (1996) *L'immeuble.* Paris: Hachette.

Diamond, M. and Hopson, J. (1998) *Magic trees of the mind.* New York: Dutton/Plume.

Dobson, A. (1998) *MFL inspected – Reflections on OFSTED inspections 1996/97.* CILT.

Doublier, M., Green, S. and Haworth, S. (1998) *On est fou du foot/Football crazy.* CILT.

Freeman, J. (1988) *Educating the very able – current international research.* OFSTED.

Gardner, H. (1983) *Frames of mind.* Basic Books.

Graham, S. (1997) *Effective language learning.* Multilingual Matters.

Green, S. (2000) *The art of war for teachers*. Teaching & Learning Publications.

Harris, V., Burch J., Jones B. and Darcy, J. (2001) *Something to say? Promoting spontaneous classroom talk*. CILT.

Holt, J. (1967) *How children learn*. Pelican.

Honnor, S. and Mascie-Taylor, H. (1982) *Tricolore Stage 3*. Pergamon Press.

Krashen, S. (1981) *Second language acquisition and second language learning*. New York: Pergamon Press.

Lee J., Buckland D. and Shaw G. (eds) (1998) *The invisible child*. CILT.

Little, D. et al (1989) *Learning foreign languages from authentic texts – theory and practice*. Authentik.

Little, D. 'Learner autonomy' in Green, S. (ed) (2000) *New perspectives on teaching and learning Modern Languages*. Multilingual Matters

Littlewood, W. (1981) *Communicative language teaching – an introduction*. CUP.

Maley, A. (1980) 'L'enseignement d'une compétence de communication: illusion du réel et réalité de l'illusion'. *Le Français dans le Monde* 153/mai–juin.

McLachlan, A. (2001) New Pathfinder 1: *Raising the standard*. CILT.

Morelock, M. and Morrison, K. (1996) *Gifted children have talents too!* Australia: Hawker Brownlow Education.

Morris, P. and Wesson, A. (1996) *Lernpunkt Deutsch 1*. Thomas Nelson.

OFSTED (2002) *Secondary subject reports 2000/01: Modern Foreign Languages*. OFSTED.

Page, B. (1992) *Letting go – taking hold*. CILT.

Rogers, B. (2002) *Classroom behaviour*. Paul Chapman Publishing.

Sadler, R. (1989) 'Formative assessment and the design of instructional systems' in *Instructional Science,* 18, 119–144.

Skehan, P. (1998) *A cognitive approach to language learning*. OUP.

Smith, A, and Call, N. (1999, revised 2000) *The ALPS approach: Accelerated learning in primary schools*. Network Educational Press.

Swarbrick, A. (ed) (1994) *Teaching Modern Languages*. OU/Routledge.

Thorndike, E. (1913) *Educational psychology – the psychology of learning*. New York: Teachers College Press.

Vygotsky, L. (1962) *Thought and language*. Cambridge Mass: MIT Press.

Wubbels, T. (1992) *Taking account of student teachers' perceptions*. Teaching and Teacher Education.

Yaiche, F. (1996) *Les simulations globales – mode d'emploi*. Paris: Hachette.

APPENDIX 1

Although the National Curriculum programme of study as a whole stresses the nature of interactive teaching, the extracts in the appendix emphasise unpredictability, independent learning, creativity and a flexible approach to language teaching. It is worth noting that there is much within the programme of study that allows the teacher great freedom to experiment, improvise and provide challenging opportunities for pupils (e.g. 'adapt language', 'strategies for dealing with the unpredictable', 'develop independence', 'personal feelings', 'use of the target language creatively and imaginatively').

These ideas are endorsed by and are in keeping with the following extracts:

The National Curriculum Programme of Study

1c Pupils should be taught how to express themselves using a range of vocabulary and structures
2d Pupils should be taught how to initiate and develop conversations
2f Pupils should be taught how to adapt language they already know for different contexts
2g Pupils should be taught strategies for dealing with the unpredictable
3d Pupils should be taught how to use dictionaries and other reference materials appropriately and effectively
3e Pupils should be taught how to develop their independence in learning and using the target language
4a Pupils should be taught about different countries and cultures by working with authentic materials in the target language
4b Pupils should be taught about different countries and cultures by considering the experiences and perspectives of people in these countries and communities

Breadth of study

5 During Key Stages 3 and 4 pupils should be taught the knowledge, skills and understanding through:
c expressing and discussing personal feelings and opinions
f using the target language creatively and imaginatively
g listening, reading or viewing for personal interest and enjoyment, as well as for information

i   working in a variety of contexts, including everyday activities, personal and social
life, the world around us, the world of work and the international world.

The Key Stage 3 National Strategy is built upon the work of the National Literacy
Strategy. It is concerned with raising educational attainment in Key Stage 3. Although
it permeates all school subjects, Modern Languages is contained within the Foundation
Subject strand and has its own framework. This is how the DfES explains its
significance:

**The KS3 National Strategy – Teaching and Learning in the Foundation Subjects
(TLF)** (taken from the DfES Standards website – **www.standards.dfes.gov.uk**)

What exactly is TLF?

TLF is one of the five strands of the Key Stage 3 National Strategy. It aims to raise
standards and to engage and motivate pupils by supporting and developing high quality
teaching and learning in the foundation subjects and RE. Its purpose is to help teachers
to become more effective in order that pupils improve in how and what they learn. It
does this by providing high quality support, illuminating best practice in generic aspects
of teaching and learning and offering subject specific guidance and materials.

What are the main principles of TLF?

The strand's principles for teaching and learning are consistent with those informing the
rest of the strategy and are summarised in the table below:

The Principle	The Action
Focus the teaching	Plan to objectives and ensure pupils know what they are
Provide challenge	Set expectations and teach to them so that pupils surpass previous levels of achievement
Make explicit concepts and conventions	Use questioning, explaining, modelling
Structure the learning	Use starters, plenaries and a clear lesson structure
Make learning active	Provide tasks in which pupils make meaning, construct knowledge and develop understanding and skills through problem-solving, investigation and enquiry
Make learning engaging and motivating	Use stimulating activities and materials
Develop well-paced lessons with high levels of interaction	Use collaborative tasks and talk for learning
Support pupils' application and independent learning	Use prompts, frames, scaffolds and targeted intervention
Build reflection	Teach pupils to think about what and how they learn and set targets for future lessons

The QCA schemes of work also provide plenty of opportunities to integrate the creative approaches of this book. Here is the French Teacher's Guide with our italics showing how this scheme of work supports the notion of creativity.

Schemes of work: Secondary Modern Foreign Languages – French Teacher's Guide

APPENDIX 2: OVERVIEW OF PROGRESSION IN THIS SCHEME OF WORK

Table 2: Skills progression

	Year 7 (Units 1–6)	Year 8 (Units 7–12)	Year 9 (Units 13–18)
Application of knowledge	pronounce parts of words or full words	read for information	use and apply knowledge of language, e.g. grammar, word families
	substitute words from memory	*unravel longer sentences in authentic texts*	increased complexity across the four attainment targets
	make sentences	*give an oral presentation*	summarise
	ask as well as answer	make longer sentences	recount
	understand instructions	recognise cognates	*use clues in text to aid understanding*
	apply knowledge, e.g. of verb paradigms, spelling rules	write a formal letter	read lengthier texts
	express simple opinions	*volunteer opinions/ reasons*	*read for pleasure*
	express simple reasons		
	early steps in independent reading		
	write an informal letter		

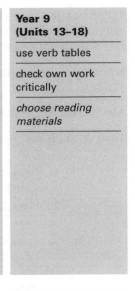

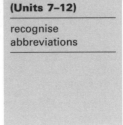

	Year 7 (Units 1–6)	Year 8 (Units 7–12)	Year 9 (Units 13–18)
Study skills and learning strategies	pronounce/ repeat	begin to use verb tables	use verb tables
	ways of learning vocabulary	increase range of classroom language	check own work critically
	make and refer to notes	refer to textbook or to work in exercise book	*choose reading materials*
	know when to ask for help	*ways to learn rules*	
	begin to deal with the unfamiliar	make notes to aid learning/ revising	
		begin to cope with the unknown/ unpredictable	

	Year 7 (Units 1–6)	Year 8 (Units 7–12)	Year 9 (Units 13–18)
Dictionary use	note differences between Fr/Eng and Eng/Fr sections	recognise abbreviations	find specific forms, e.g. feminine, past participle, irregular, plural
	how to find gender		*choose between alternatives*
	verb in infinitive		

Finally, even exam board specifications can provide support for a creative approach when we look closely at their aims and objectives. This extract is taken from the GCSE: AQA Specification A for 2003 French (3651) (our emphasis shown in italics).

A course based on this specification should encourage candidates to:

a. develop understanding of the spoken and written forms of French *in a range of contexts;*

b. develop the ability to communicate effectively in French, through both the spoken and written word, *using a range of vocabulary and structures;*

c. develop knowledge and understanding of the grammar of French, and the *ability to apply it;*

d. apply their knowledge and understanding *in a variety of relevant contexts* which reflect their previous learning and maturity;

e. develop knowledge and understanding of countries and communities where French is spoken;

f. develop positive attitudes to French learning;

g. provide a *suitable foundation for further study* and/or practical use of French.

APPENDIX 2
French version for the grid – setting the story in a village

With the grid on the OHP, you make the following three requests in French:

- *Donne-moi un numéro: 2*
- *Donne-moi une lettre: A*
- *Donne-moi une couleur: Rouge*

Stage 4

Le Village

You then make the following suggestions:

 la rivière

 les écoles

 les magasins

 les églises

You then ask a series of questions to build up the context more fully:

- *Quel est le nom de cette rivière?*
- *Quels sonts les magasins?*
- *C'est une école primaire?*
- *C'est une église catholique?*

These questions can go on for as long as the teacher feels that the class are with him or her and are contributing actively to the process. There are no right answers, but each answer is accepted and added to the whole picture with the teacher making any linguistic adjustments that are deemed necessary.

Let us take just one shop as an example: A2.

- *C'est la boulangerie.*
- *Qui est le boulanger?*

- *A-t-il une femme?*
- *Comment s'appelle-t-elle?*
- *Ils ont des enfants?*
- *Combien?*
- *Ils ont quel âge?*
- *Comment s'appellent-ils?*
- *Est-ce qu'ils vont à l'école dans le village?*
- *Comment vont-ils à l'école?*

A pupil may well ask for help with a question such as: *Comment dit-on en français:* 'forest'?

Spanish version for the grid – setting the story in a village

Stage 2

With the grid on the OHP, you make the following three requests in Spanish:

- *Dame un número: 2*
- *Dame una letra: A*
- *Dame un color: Rojo*

Stage 4

El pueblo

 el río

 los colegios

 las tiendas

 las iglesias

- *¿Cómo se llama el río?*
- *¿Qué tiendas hay?*
- *¿Es una escuela?*
- *¿Es una iglesia católica?*

Let us take just one shop as an example: A2.

- *Es la panadería.*
- *¿Quién es el panadero?*
- *¿Está casado?*
- *¿Cómo se llama su esposa?*
- *¿Tienen hijos?*
- *¿Cuántos?*
- *¿Cuántos años tienen?*
- *¿Cómo se llaman?*
- *¿Van a la escuela?*
- *¿Cómo llegan a la escuela?*

At some point a pupil is going to ask: *¿Cómo se dice en español* 'forest'?

APPENDIX 3
First names

French

Male

Achille, Adam, Barthélémy, Basile, Cédric, César, Charles, Damien, Daniel, Edmond, Édouard, Fabien, Fabrice, Gabin, Gabriel, Henri, Hervé, Ignace, Jacob, Jacques, Jean, Laurent, Léon, Marc, Marcel, Nicolas, Noël, Odilon, Olivier, Pascal, Paul, Philippe, Raoul, Raphaël, Samuel, Sébastien, Théodore, Thierry, Valentin, Valère, Victor, Xavier, Yves, Yvon, Zacharie

Female

Adélaïde, Adèle, Babette, Barbara, Camille, Candice, Danielle, Delphine, Éléonore, Éliane, Fabienne, Félicie, Gabrielle, Georgette, Hélène, Héloise, Irène, Isabelle, Jacqueline, Jeanne, Laure, Laurence, Madeleine, Magali, Nadège, Nathalie, Odile, Olive, Paméla, Pascale, Régine, Reine, Sabine, Sandrine, Thérèse, Valérie, Véronique, Yolande, Yvette, Zoé

German

Male

Achim, Adelbert, Arnim, Benno, Berthold, Bruno, Christoph, Dietmar, Dietrich, Erwin, Frank, Friedrich, Gunter, Hans-Peter, Heinz, Ingo, Joachim, Jens, Karl, Klaus, Matthias, Oskar, Otto, Rainer, Ralf, Siegfried, Stefan, Thomas, Tobias, Udo, Ulf, Volker, Walter, Wolfgang

Female

Annike, Astrid, Beate, Brigitte, Carla, Christa, Claudia, Dagmar, Dorothee, Elke, Frauke, Gitte, Grethe, Hanna, Heidrun, Ilse, Ingrid, Jessica, Jutta, Karin, Kerstin, Lieselotte, Marike, Martina, Nina, Olga, Petra, Regina, Roswitha, Sara, Sabine

Spanish

Male

Alfonso, Antonio, Carlos, David, Eduardo, Francisco, Ignacio, José, Juan, Julio, Luis, Manuel, Pablo, Patricio, Pedro, Ramón, Ricardo, Roberto, Sebastián, Salvador, Tomás, Víctor

Female

Alicia, Ana, Begoña, Carmen, Cristina, Elena, Francisca, Gloria, Inmaculada, Isabel, Juanita, Julia, Luisa, María, Marisol, Marta, Nuria, Paula, Rosa, Susana, Teresa, Yolanda

APPENDIX 4
The 3–2–1 game – suggestions for vocabulary that might help

German

1 word	2 words	3 words
ja	na ja	wie war es?
nein	bis bald	wie heißt er?
ach	wieso denn?	wohin gehst du?
nee	und dann?	du liebe Zeit
na	ja und?	du meine Güte
was!	Moment mal	sonst noch etwas?
wer?	warum nicht?	sag ruhig was
wo?	wo denn?	bist du böse?
wann?	wie denn?	das kannst du
wie?	siehst du?	nein, nicht möglich
wieso?	ach nein	um Gottes Willen
warum?	musst du?	was meinst du?
weshalb?	kannst du?	wo warst du?
so	willst du?	in der Kirche
nicht	du sollst	in der Kneipe
doch	wann denn?	kommst du mit?
Quatsch	geh doch	du darfst nicht
Unsinn	im Kino	um zwei Uhr
meinetwegen	im Park	geh ins Bett
sofort	ich friere	hast du Hunger?
also	also denn	wie geht's?

French

1 word	2 words	3 words
bof	ça alors	avec mon ami
alors	zut alors	papa a peur
et	avec qui?	oui ça va
quoi?	pourquoi pas?	tout de suite
quand?	en ville	juste à côté
comment?	avec Henri	à quelle heure?
zut	tu dis	dans le cinéma
où?	ça va	devant la gare
qui?	et alors?	derrière la maison
pourquoi?	mais, pourquoi?	dis pas ça
mais	mais, comment?	où étais-tu?
maintenant	quelle surprise!	va au lit
fantastique!	quelle catastrophe!	j'ai faim
splendide!	mais si	j'ai soif
superbe!	mais oui	j'ai peur
affreux!	sans Henri	oh là là!
bonsoir	cinq fois	c'est affreux!

Spanish

1 word	2 words	3 words
¿Pués?	¿Por qué?	Con mi amigo
¿Qué?	Ahora mismo	Poco a poco
¡Hola!	Muy bien	¿Qué me dices?
¿Dónde?	¿Con quién?	¿A qué hora?
¿Cómo?	No quiero	Son las tres
¿Cuándo?	Cuando pueda	Tengo mucho sueño
Ahora	Con Isabel	Delante del hotel
Tranquilo	¿Adónde vas?	¡No me digas!
Despacio	Con paraguas	A las dos
Paciencia	Sin abrigo	¿Qué hay, mamá?
¡Hombre!	En Madrid	No tengo dinero
Enfrente	Bien, gracias	En la calle
Discúlpame	Lo siento	No me apetece
Pero	¡Qué horror!	No hay derecho
¡Espléndido!	Te quiero	¡A la cama!
¿Quién?	¡Vaya sorpresa!	Buenas noches, mamá
¡Caramba!	¡Ni hablar!	¿Quién es ésta?